D1600408

A VIRGINIA GIRL IN THE CIVIL WAR

Being a Record of the Actual Experiences of the Wife of a Confederate Officer

Collected and Edited By Myrta Lockett Avary

THE NARRATIVE PRESS

TRUE FIRST-PERSON HISTORICAL ACCOUNTS

The text for this book was obtained from an original edition published in February 1903 by D. Appleton and Company, New York.

The Narrative Press
P.O. Box 2487, Santa Barbara, California 93120 U.S.A.
Telephone: (800) 315-9005 Web: www.narrativepress.com

ISBN 1-58976-252-5 (Paperback)

Produced in the United States of America

CONTENTS

Introduction

THIS history was told over the tea-cups. One winter, in the South, I had for my neighbor a gentle, little brown-haired lady, who spent many evenings at my fireside, as I at hers, where with bits of needlework in our hands we gossiped away as women will. I discovered in her an unconscious heroine, and her Civil War experiences made ever an interesting topic. Wishing to share with others the reminiscences she gave me, I seek to present them here in her own words. Just as they stand, they are, I believe, unique, possessing at once the charm of romance and the veracity of history. They supply a graphic, if artless, picture of the social life of one of the most interesting and dramatic periods of our national existence. The stories were not related in strict chronological sequence, but I have endeavored to arrange them in that way. Otherwise, I have made as few changes as possible. Out of deference to the wishes of living persons, her own and her husband's real names have been suppressed and others substituted; in the case of a few of their close personal friends, and of some whose names would not be of special historical value, the same plan has been followed.

Those who read this book are admitted to the sacred councils of close friends, and I am sure they will turn with reverent fingers these pages of a sweet and pure woman's life - a life on which, since those fireside talks of ours, the Death-Angel has set his seal.

Memoirs and journals written not because of their historical or political significance, but because they are to the writer the natural expression of what life has meant to him in the moment of living, have a value entirely apart from literary quality. They bring us close to the human soul - the human soul in undress. We find ourselves without preface or apology in personal, intimate relation with whatever makes the yesterday, to-day, to-morrow of the writer. When this current of events and conditions is impelled and directed by a vital

and formative period in the history of a nation, we have only to follow its course to see what history can never show us, and what fiction can unfold to us only in part - how the people thought, felt, and lived who were not making history, or did not know that they were.

This is the essential value of A Virginia Girl in the Civil War: it shows us simply, sincerely, and unconsciously what life meant to an American woman during the vital and formative period of American history. That this American woman was also a Virginian with all a Virginian's love for Virginia and loyalty to the South, gives to her record of those days that are still "the very fiber of us" a fidelity rarely found in studies of local color. Meanwhile, her grateful affection for the Union soldiers, officers and men, who served and shielded her, should lift this story to a place beyond the pale of sectional prejudice.

Myrta Lockett Avary.

New York, November 1, 1902.

Chapter I

HOME LIFE IN A SOUTHERN HARBOR

MANY years ago I heard a prominent lawyer of Baltimore, who had just returned from visit to Charleston, say that the Charlestonians were so in the habit of antedating everything with the Civil War that when he commented to one of them upon the beauty of the moonlight on the Battery, his answer was, "You should have seen it before the war." I laughed, as everybody else did; but since then I have more than once caught myself echoing the sentiment of that Charleston citizen to visitors who exclaimed over the social delights of Norfolk. For really they know nothing about it - that is, about the real Norfolk.Nobody does who can not remember, as I do, when her harbor was covered with shipping which floated flags of all nations, and her society was the society of the world. Milicent and I - there were only the two of us - were as familiar with foreign colors as with our own Red, White, and Blue, and happily grew up unconscious that a title had any right of precedence superior to that of youth, good breeding, good looks, and agreeability. That all of these gave instant way to the claims of age was one of the unalterable tenets handed down from generation to generation, and punctiliously observed in our manner and address to the older servants. The "uncle" and "aunty" and "mammy" that fall so oddly upon the ears of the present generation were with Southern children and young people the "straight and narrow" path that separated gentle birth and breeding from the vulgar and ignorant.

My girlhood was a happy one. My father was an officer of the Bank of Virginia, and, according to the custom that obtained, he lived over the bank. His young assistant, Walter H. Taylor (afterward adjutant to General R. E. Lee), was like a brother to Milicent and me. Father's position and means, and the personal charm that left him and my mother cherished memories in Norfolk till to-day, drew around us a cultivated and cosmopolitan society. Our lives were made up of dance and song and moonlit sails. There were the Atlantic Ocean, the Roads, the bay, the James and Elizabeth rivers, meeting at our very door. And there were admirals, commodores, and captains whose good ships rode these waters, and who served two sovereign - the nation whose flag they floated and a slim Virginia maiden. In all the gatherings, formal and informal, under our roof, naval and military uniforms predominated. Many men who later distinguished themselves in the Federal and Confederate armies, sat around our board and danced in our parlors; others holding high places in Eastern and European courts were numbered among our friends and acquaintances.

Some years after Commodore Perry through a skilful mixture of gunpowder and diplomacy had opened the ports of Japan to the commerce of all nations, Ito and Inouye - not then counts - had brought into existence an organized Japanese navy which sailed out of these same ports to the harbors of the world on tours of inspection. One of my most vivid memories is of the Japanese squadron which lay at anchor in our harbor, of the picturesque dress and manners of these Eastern strangers, and the polished courtesy of the two men whose names are now a part of history.

But the handsomest sailors I ever saw were the Prussians. When the Prussian navy was in its infancy two Prussian vessels, the frigate Gaefion and a corvette, dropped anchor in Norfolk harbor; they, too, were visiting the ports of different nations on tours of inspection. All the officers on these vessels, including the midshipmen, were noblemen, and all of them were magnificent- looking men. Then, too, their brilliant uniforms and the state and ceremony with which they invested every-day life made them altogether charming to a young, romantic girl. I shall never forget how they used to enter the room. They would appear in full regimentals, march in military form, the frigate's captain in command, and salute Milicent before they permitted themselves to talk, dance, and sing. Upon leaving, the same order was observed. They went out into the hall, donned their hats, sword-belts, and swords, returned, saluted, and withdrew in military form. At this time I was a little girl who played on the piano for grown-up people to dance. On formal occasions we had military bands, but for the every-evening dance my playing did well enough. When the Prussians were our guests, one of them always sat by me while I played. Baron von der Golz, since Admiral of the German navy, was the gentleman who was oftenest kind enough to turn over my music. I play now, for my children to dance, a Prussian galop he taught me, with some of the music I played for those officers, and some which they used to play when they took my place at the piano that I might have my share of the dancing. Another Prussian officer of whom I was very fond was Count van Monts, afterward Admiral of the German navy, Von der Golz succeeding at his death.

I shall never forget the day my Prussian friends sailed away. From the roof of our residence over the bank, there was a good view of the harbor and river: Milicent, Emily Conway, and a number of girls who wanted to see the last of the gallant, handsome Prussians went up on the roof, and I was permitted to go with them. We turned our spy-glasses on their ships as they sailed toward Hampton Roads, and there were our friends on deck, their glasses turned upon the housetop where we stood in the full glare of the midday sun. Even I was visible to them. Milicent placed me in front of our spy-glass, and I looked through and singled out Baron von Golz, to whom I waved my handkerchief vigorously. A little snowstorm fluttered on the deck, and the baron not only waved, but saluted. According to the fashion of the time, young ladies wore low-necked dresses in the middle of the day - never, however, at any hour, so low as ladies at the opera wear them now. Milicent and her friends who went to the housetop were bare- necked, and the sun blistered their throats and shoulders; and mother had to bathe Milicent with buttermilk all the afternoon to make her presentable for the dance that night, which, by special permission, Count von Monts attended, coming up from Fortress Monroe to escort Milicent. They made a pretty picture when they danced their last dance together. The Count would not permit their friendship to cease with that last dance, and a correspondence was long kept up between them. At parting, she gave him her little Catholic prayer- book with her name on the fly-leaf, and years after, when revisiting Norfolk, he had that prayer- book and tried to find her; but times were changed, and Norfolk no more our home. Many a titled sailor sought my sister's favor, but in our day Virginia's daughters, undazzled by coronets, were content to wed Virginia's sons.

The almost limitless hospitality of those days made all the sharper the distinction between "open house" and open hand. In the forties, the reserve of the American girl was more like that of her English sister than it is at the present day. Society did not sanction the freedom which it countenances now. The gentlewoman of the old South was a past mistress in the art of tact, but had little knowledge or practice in it to further her own private ends. Its office, as she understood it, was to relieve painful situations not her own, to contribute to the comfort and pleasure of others. To rid herself of a disagreeable third person to secure a tête-à-tête with a lover was not within its province. Lovers had to make their own opportunities - indeed it was not her part even to conceive that they wanted to make opportunities. Taking all this into consideration, the freedom with which Southern children entered into the social life must have often made them thorns in the flesh of their elders. I have often wondered since those happy days if my favorites among my sister's visitors did not find me a great nuisance in spite of the caresses they lavished upon me.

The New Year's reception of that period was not an afternoon and evening affair. It began in the morning and lasted all day; it meant pretty girls fluttering in laces and ribbons and feathers and sparkling with jewel and smiles; stately matrons who, however beautiful and young they were, never indulged even in the innocent coquetry that neither deceives a man nor wounds a woman - the married belle was unknown to Virginia; and gallant men, young and old, ready to die for them or live for them; it meant the good things to eat for which Virginia is famous, and, I am sorry to say, often more than enough of good things to drink. I remember one of these New Year's days when the ardor of my affections prevented a young officer who had come to bid us good-by from exchanging a word with anybody unhampered by my close attendance. I was brimful of nine-year-old love for him. I proposed to him and was promptly accepted; I made him drink punch with me dipped from the old punch-bowl that had been presented to father by the military companies of Norfolk, and I told him how Admiral Tucker had made the presentation with flags flying and bands playing and wine flowing, and how the admiral tried to ride his horse up the front steps into the house, and how the sober animal wisely and firmly refused to perfom the feat Through a long day he did not once escape me. This young officer was Lieutenant John L. Worden. He was one of the gallant "boys in blue" who made my sister's girlhood happy. A most charming gentleman he was, and everybody in my father's house loved him.

Another young sailor - the handsomest of them all, whom everybody in my father's house loved - was Captain Warren. How well I remember that evening when the order came bidding him report at once to his ship, which was to set forth on a long cruise in Eastern waters! Shall I ever forget the look in his eyes as he turned them upon Milicent! How beautiful she was that night! How gracious and sweet, how greatly to be desired! And how many desired her!

Milicent had been married several years and I was in the raptures of my first winter in society when my father died, and mother decided that we should leave Norfolk - Norfolk where river and bay and ocean had sung our cradle-songs - and go to Petersburg to live. In this day of independent women it sounds absurd to say that it was scarcely considered wise or delicate for women to live without the protection of a male relative in the house, and to add that as far as possible they were shielded from the burden of business responsibilities.

Uncle Henry considered it imperative that we should be under his care; he could not come to Norfolk, so we went to him. We could scarcely have been strangers anywhere in Virginia, and in Petersburg we had many friends. The Lees and the Randolphs, the Pegrams and the Pages, the Stringfellows, the Hamiltons, the Witherspoons, the Bannisters, the Donnans, the Dunlops, and a score of others made it easy to exercise the genius for friendship which in Virginia hands down that relation from generation to generation.

It was in Petersburg that my trousseau was made. Much of it was the work and embroidery of loving, light-hearted girls whose feet were set to music and dancing, and most of it was worn by women who trod instead fields red with the blood of their friends and kinsmen. During the long, dreary years in which the Northern ports were closed, and the South clothed itself as best it could, or went in rags, that trousseau constituted my sole outfit, and it reinforced the wardrobes of some comrades in war and want.

Chapter II

How I Met Dan Grey

"HAVE you met Dan Grey?"

Charlie Murray and I were galloping along a country road.

"I haven't, Charlie. I met his brother Dick in Norfolk, and didn't like him at all."

"Well, Nell, you'd like Dan - everybody does. I wonder you haven't met him. Dan never fails to meet every pretty girl that comes here."

I had heard that before. Indeed, I had heard a great deal about Dan Grey that made me long to get even with him. Everybody had a way of speaking as if Petersburg wasn't Petersburg with Dan Grey left out.

"You ought to meet Dan Grey," Charlie repeated.

"I don't think so," I rapped out. "I think I can get along very nicely without meeting Dan Grey" - Dan Grey seemed to be getting along very nicely without meeting me - "I know as many nice men now as I have time to see."

So I dismissed Dan, whipped up my horse, and raced Charlie along the old Jerusalem Plank Road - that historic thoroughfare by which the Union troops first threatened Petersburg, and near which Fort Hell and Fort Damnation are still visible. We ran our horses past the old brick church, built of bricks brought from England to erect a place of worship for the aristocratic colonists, past the quiet graves in Blandford; and turning our horses into Washington Street, slackened their pace and, chatting merrily the while, rode slowly into the city toward the golden sunset. A few years later I was to run along this street in abject terror from bursting shells.

"You ought to meet Dan Grey."

It came from George Van B this time. George was the poet laureate of our set. Afterward he was Colonel Van B, and as gallant a soldier as ever faced shot and shell. I had been playing an accompaniment for him; he was singing a popular ditty of the day, "Sweet Nellie is by my Side"; I wheeled around on the piano-stool and faced him.

"What is the matter with that man? He must be a curiosity?"

"He is just the nicest fellow in town,"

George asserted with mingled resentment and amusement.

"He must be something extraordinary. One would think there was just one man in town and that his name was Dan Grey."

Before the week was out I heard it again. This time it was Willie. He spoke oracularly, and as if he were broaching an original idea. Page, the best dancer in our set, repeated the recommendation, looking as if I were quite out of the swim in not knowing Dan Grey. (If Governor - reads this chapter, will he please overlook the familiar use of his name? Boys and girls who have played mumble-peg together and snowballed each other, do not attach handles to each other's names until they are more thoroughly grown up than we were then.)

"I am sure it must be my duty to meet Dan Grey," I said gravely. "I am continually being told that I 'ought to meet Dan Grey' just as I might be told that I ought to go to church."

"Dan isn't a bit like a church, Nell," laughed Willie. "But he is a splendid fellow, generous to a fault - and then, you know, Dan is the handsomest man in town."

"Oh, no!" I retorted, "I left the handsomest man in town in Norfolk."

I can't begin to tell how terribly tired I got of "You ought to meet Dan Grey," "Haven't you met Dan Grey?" Evidently

Dan Grey was in no hurry to meet me. I knew that he was the toast of our set and that he ignored me as completely as if I were not in it - and I had never been ignored before. I also knew, without being continually told, that he was a broad-shouldered, magnificent-looking fellow, fair-haired, blue-eyed, and "the handsomest man in town." My girl friends talked about him almost as much as the men did. And I did not even know the lion! I took great pains not to want to know him. I impressed it upon Willie and Charlie and George and the rest that they were not to bring Dan Grey to see me.

"Why, what will we say if he asks us to bring him? You are unreasonable, Nell. How did you ever pick up such a prejudice against Dan? Nobody can object to Dan Grey. If he asks any of us to bring him, I don't know what we can do."

"Oh, of course you can't be rude. If you are asked to bring him, you will have to do as you are asked, but I don't think you will be asked. I'm sure I hope you won't, for I have heard of Dan Grey until I am sick of the very name."

Meanwhile I resolved privately if I ever did lay my hands on Dan Grey I would wreak a full vengeance. He says that I have done it.

A Catholic fair was to be held in Petersburg, but as dearly as we loved Father Mulvey (all Petersburg loved him), and as much as we longed to do everything possible for our poor little Church of St. Joseph, we could not go to the fair rooms and sell things and make merry. We were in deep mourning; mother said that our going was out of the question. Then her old friend, Mrs. Winton, came out to persuade and convince.

"I really can not let the girls go," mother protested. "They can make fancy articles and send them to the fair, or do any home work that you can put them to; we are willing to help just as much as we can. I will send pickled oysters and shrimp salad after my Norfolk recipes, and cake and cream and anything you like that I can make."

"We want the oysters and the salad and the cake and everything else you choose to send, but above all things we want the girls. I didn't come here for your pickled oysters and shrimp salad, if they are the best I ever tasted. I want Milicent and Nell - I want Nell for my booth and Milicent for Mrs. Lynn's. Mrs. Lynn has set her heart on Milicent - but, there! Mrs. Lynn may do her own begging. Do let me have Nell."

"My dear, I don't see how I can."

"Oh, you must! We really need them. You know how few girls there are in our little congregation."

Mother was too good a Catholic not to yield - Milicent and I were given over to the cause of St. Joseph's.

"But they are to work, not to amuse themselves," she stipulated. "They are not to promenade - just to stand behind tables and sell things."

"Just send them," pleaded Mrs. Winton. "I'll promise not to let them enjoy themselves. I'll keep Nell busy, and Mrs. Lynn will do her duty by Milicent."

But work is fun when you are young enough, and there was plenty of both in getting the booths ready. The old Library Hall on Bollingbrook Street was a gay and busy scene for several days before it was formally opened to the public who came to spend money and make merry.

On one never-forgotten morning the hall was filled with matrons and maidens weaving festoons of pine-beard, running cedar, and ivy. I had purposely donned my worst dress, and was sitting on the floor Turkish fashion, with evergreens heaped around me, when I saw a party of gentlemen entering the hall.

I tried to sink out of sight, but they saw me, demolished my barricade, and began to tease me. The quartet were Charlie Murray, George Van B, Willie, and Page. Behind them came a fifth gentleman, and before this fifth gentleman and I knew what was happening we were being presented to each other. And that is how I met Dan Grey - sitting on the floor in my shabbiest dress and half hidden by evergreens. I soon had the whole party hard at work festooning the hall, and what a good, if late, laborer, Dan Grey made in my vineyard!

"You see how useful I am," he said - he was standing on a box and I was handing up wreaths of cedar which he was arranging on the wall. "Now, why didn't you let me come to see you?"

"Me?" I asked in utter bewilderment.

"Yes, 'me'!"

"Why, I never had a thing to do with your not coming to see me."

He gave George, Charlie, and Willie a withering look.

"I reckon somebody else didn't want me to."

The boys looked dumfounded.

"I heard," said Dan from his box, "that you didn't want me to come to see you, that you had an unaccountable prejudice against me because you didn't like Dick, that you asked all your friends by no means to bring me to see you."

I was as mad as I could be with George, Willie, and Charlie.

"Why," I said, "you are not your brother Dick. And then, I don't dislike Dick at all."

Again the trio looked at me as if they doubted the evidence of their senses.

"Nell, what did you tell such a story for?" George asked me privately later.

"Why, I didn't tell any story at all," I declared. "He isn't his brother Dick, is he? And I don't dislike Dick now."

The night of the fair I wore a black bombazine, cut low in the neck and with long angel sleeves falling away from my arms above the elbow to the hem of my dress, and around my neck a band of black velvet with a black onyx cross. I sat or stood behind Mrs. Winton's booth, and Mr. Grey haunted the booth all the evening, and bought quantities of things he had no use for.

After the fair he saw me or reminded me of his existence in some way every day. Mother took me, about this time, on a visit to some cousins in Birdville, and every day Mr. Grey rode out on Dare Devil, the horse that he was to ride into his first fight. There was another fair. I went in from Birdville to help, and had the same cotcrie of assistants. "Ben Bolt" was a great favorite then. It was a new song and divided honors with "Sweet Nellie is by my Side." My assistants used to sit on a goods box that was later to be converted into an ornamental stand, and sing, "O don't you Remember Sweet Alice, Ben Bolt?"

Well, to make a long story short - as Dan and I did - we were married in exactly four months and a half from the day on which he was introduced to me as I sat cross-legged among the evergreens; and when Willie and George and Charlie came up to congratulate us, every wretch of them said, "Didn't I tell you you ought to meet Dan Grey?"

Chapter III

The First Days Of The Confederacy

SOON after my marriage my brother-in-law moved to Baltimore, and my mother decided to go with Milicent and her little boy. I had never really been separated from them before; I was only seventeen, a spoiled child, but though I loved them dearly, after the first I scarcely missed them. I had my husband, and ah! how happy we were - how glad we both were that I had met Dan Grey!

We did not go to housekeeping at once. In the first place, I did not know anything about housekeeping and I didn't want Dan to find it out; in the second place, we wanted to look around before we settled upon a house; and in the third, and what was to me the smallest place, the country was in a very unsettled condition.

The question of State's rights and secession was being pressed home to Virginia.

The correspondence between the commission at Washington and Mr. Seward was despatched to Richmond, and Richmond is but twenty miles from Petersburg. There were mutterings that each day grew louder, signs and portents that we refused to believe. Local militia were organizing and drilling - getting ready to answer the call should it come. Not that the people seriously thought that it would come. They believed, as they hoped, that something would be done to prevent war; that statesmen, North and South, would combine to save the Union; that, at any rate, we should be saved from bloodshed. As for those others who prophesied and prayed for it, who wanted thc vials of God's wrath uncorked, they got what they wanted. Their prayers were answered; the land was drenched in blood. But for the most of us - the Virginians whom I knew - we did not, we would not believe that brothers could war with brothers.

Then something happened that drove the truth home to our hearts. The guns of Sumter spoke - war was upon us. But not for long; the differences would be adjusted.

Sumter fell, Virginia seceded. Still we befooled ourselves. There would be a brief campaign, victory, and peace. North and South, we looked for anything but what came - those four long years of bloody agony; North and South were each sure of victory. In Virginia, where the courage and endurance of starving men were to stand the test of weary months and years, we scoffed at the idea that there would be any real fighting. If there should be, for Virginia who had never known the shadow of defeat, defeat was impossible.

One day my brother-in-law, Dick, walked in.

"I've come to tell you good-by, Nell - I'm off to-morrow."

"Where?"

"Norfolk."

"What for?"

"Infantry ordered there. The Rifles go down to-night, the Grays to-morrow."

I looked serious, and Dick laughed.

"Don't bother, Nell, we'll be back in a few days. There won't be any fighting." Dick was a good-looking fellow, and I liked him much better than I had once said I did. He was the dandy of the family, and on the present occasion was glorious in a new uniform.

"Dick," I said, "please don't get in a fight and get shot."

"Not if I can help it, Nell! There won't be any fighting. We're going to protect Norfolk, you know. Just going there to be on the spot if we're needed, I suppose."

He went away laughing, but I wasn't convinced. When Dan came, I was almost too weak with fear to ask the question that was on my tongue.

"Is Norfolk to be bombarded?"

"No, I think not," he spoke cheerily. "The boys will be back in a few days."

Oh, I hoped they would! Many of my friends were among "the boys."

"Do - do you think your company will have to go?"

I was only seventeen; mother and Milicent were away; my young husband was my life.

"The cavalry have not been ordered out," he said. "I don't think we will be sent for.

Cheer up, Nell! The boys will be back in a few days, and won't we have a high old time welcoming them home!"

Dick had broken it to me gently. All the infantry went down together. Soon after my husband came in, looking very pale and quiet.

"Dan," I said, "I know what it is."

"The cavalry are ordered to Norfolk," he said in a low voice. "It's only a few days' parting, little wife. I don't think there will be any fighting. Be brave, my darling."

I had thrown myself into his arms with great cry.

"I can't, Dan! I can't let you go!"

He did not speak. He only held me close to his breast.

"Mother and Milicent are gone," I cried, "and I can't let you leave me to go and be killed! I couldn't let you go if they were here."

There was silence for a little while, then he said:

"I belong to you, little wife - I leave it to you what I shall do. Shall I stay behind, a traitor and a coward? Or shall I go with my company and do my duty?"

I couldn't speak for tears. I felt how hard his heart beat against mine.

"Poor wife!" he said, "poor little child!"

When I spoke, I felt as if I were tearing my heart out by

the roots.

"I - I - must - let - you - go!"

"That is my own brave girl. Never mind, Nell, I will make you proud of your soldier!"

"Oh, Dan! Dan!" I sobbed, "I don't want to be proud of you! I just don't want you to get hurt! I don't want you to go if I could help it - but I can't! I don't want fame or glory! I want you!"

He smoothed my hair with slow touches, and was silent. Then he spoke again, trying to comfort me with those false hopes all fed on.

"I still doubt if there will be any fighting. But if there is, I must be in it. I can't be a coward There! there! Nellie, don't cry! I hope for peace. The North and the South both want peace. You will laugh at all of this, Nell, when we come back from Norfolk without striking a blow!"

"Dan, let me go with you."

"Dear, I can't. How could you travel around, with only a knapsack, like a soldier?"

"Try me. I am to be a soldier's wife."

I was swallowing my sobs, sniffling, blowing my nose, and trying to look brave all at once. Instead of looking brave, I must have looked very comical, for Dan burst out laughing. The next moment we were silent again. The chimes of St. Paul's rang out upon the air. It was neither Sabbath nor saint's day. We knew what the bells were ringing for. Not only St. Paul's chimes, but the bells of all the churches had become familiar signals calling us to labor as sacred as worship. Sewing machines had been carried into the churches, and the sacred buildings had become depots for bolts of cloth, linen, and flannel. Nothing could be heard in them for days but the click of machines, the tearing of cloth, the ceaseless murmur of voices questioning, and voices directing the work. Old and young were busy. Some were tearing flannel into lengths for shirts and cutting out havelocks and knapsacks. And some were tearing linen into strips and rolling it for bandages ready to the surgeon's hand. Others were picking linen into balls of lint.

"I must go make you some clothes," I said, getting up from Dan's knee.

"But I have plenty," he said.

"It doesn't matter. I must make you some more - like the others."

Before the war was over I had learned to make clothes out of next to nothing, but that morning, except for fancy work, I had never sewed a stitch in my life. I could embroider anything from an altar cloth to an initial in the corner of a handkerchief, but to make a flannel shirt was beyond my comprehension. Make it, however, I could and would. I ever hinted to Dan that I didn't know how, or I was determined that nobody but me should make his army shirts - I must sew them with my own fingers. I went down town and bought the finest, softest flannel I could find. Then I was at my wits' ends. I looked at the flannel and I looked at the scissors. Time was flying. I picked up my flannel and ran to consult my neighbor, Mrs. Cuthbert. She showed me how to cut and fashion my shirts, and I made them beautifully, feather-stitching all the seams.

Next day came and Dan made me buckle on his sword.

"If you stay long in Norfolk may I come?" I sobbed.

Poor Dan didn't know what to say.

"I'm a soldier's wife," I said with a mighty effort to look it. "I can travel with a knapsack - and," with a sob, "I can - keep - from crying."

"I'm going to have you with me if possible. There! little wife, don't cry, or you'll make a fool of me. Be brave, Nell. That's it! I'm proud of you."

But there was a tremor in his voice all the same. He put me gently away from him and went out, and I lay down on the sofa and cried as if my heart would break. But not for long. Captain Jeter's wife came for me; her eyes were red with weeping, but she was trying to smile. We were to go to the public leave-taking - there would be time enough for tears afterward. Everybody was on the streets to see the troops go off, and I took my stand with the others and watched as the cavalry rode past us. We kept our handkerchiefs waving all the time our friends were riding by, and when we saw our husbands and brothers we tried to cheer, but our voices were husky. The last thing I saw of my husband he was wringing the hand of an old friend who was not going, tears were streaming down his cheeks and he was saying, "For God's sake, take care of my wife."

They were gone, all gone, infantry and cavalry, the flower of the city. But they would be back in a few days, of that we were sure - and some of them never came back again.

I was in a city of mourning and dread, but my own suspense measured by days was not long, though it seemed an age to me then. A week had not passed when I got a telegram from Dan:

"Come to Norfolk. We are camped near there."

It was near train time when I got it. I snatched up my satchel, put in a comb and brush and tooth-brush - not even an extra handkerchief - and almost ran to the depot. I could not have carried all my clothes, I know, for part of them were with the laundress, and packing a trunk would have taken time; but why on earth I did not put a few more articles into my satchel I can not tell. It is a matter of history, however, that I only took those I have named. The first thing Dan did was to get me some handkerchiefs.

"Why, Nell," he said, "you are taking this thing of being a soldier's wife too seriously."

It was delightful to be in my old home once more. Friends and kindred crowded around me, the river and bay and ocean sang my old cradle-songs to me again, and, above all, Dan was near and came in from camp as often as he could. Then he was ordered away to Suffolk, which is twenty miles from Norfolk, and there, of course, he could not ride in to see me. But that was not so bad as it might have been. I could hear from him regularly, he had not yet been in any actual engagement, my fears were subsiding, or I was getting accustomed to them. I had, of course, telegraphed to Petersburg for my baggage and had made myself as comfortable as possible. An old uncle had taken it into his head to become quite fond of me, and altogether I was very far from unhappy. This uncle was eccentric and had eccentric ways of comforting me when I had the blues.

"Why, Nellie, my dear," he used to say, "you ought to be playing dolls, and here you are a wife, and if Dan gets killed you will be a widow."

On the heels of which cheerful observation his despatch came from Suffolk:

"Come by next train. Dan slightly hurt. "Jack"

When I got to Suffolk four of the company met me.

"Don't be alarmed, Miss Nell," said the great fellows, sympathy and desire to cheer me blending in their eyes. "Dan will pull through all right."

Then Jack Carrington took me aside and explained as gently and tenderly as if he had been my brother:

"It happened yesterday, Miss Nell, but we wouldn't let you know because there was no way for you to get here then. We thought it wouldn't be so hard on you if we waited and sent the telegram just before train time. Your uncle got one before you did, but we told him not to tell you till just before train time, and he wired us back to tell you ourselves, that he couldn't tell you. Dan is getting all right now - he'll soon get well, Miss Nell, indeed he will. But the doctor said I must warn you - Miss Nell, you must be brave, you see - or I can't tell you at all. The doctor said I mustn't let you go in there unless you were perfectly calm. The wound is nothing at all, Miss Nell."

Poor Jack was almost as unnerved as I was. He mopped my face with a wet handkerchief, and made somebody bring me some brandy.

But the words ringing in my head, "A soldier's wife,"

pulled me together more than the brandy, and I made Jack go on.

"It's nothing but his arm. We were out on vidette duty yesterday and we got shot into. You see, Miss Nell, you must be brave or I can't tell you!"

I pulled myself together again and insisted that I was brave.

"You don't look like it, Miss Nell. I declare you don't."

"But I am. See now."

Jack didn't seem to see, but he went on, looking scared himself all the time.

"The real trouble was Dare Devil. You see, after Dan's arm got hurt - I wish it had been me or George who had caught that shot. but, hang the luck! it was Dan. You know Dare Devil's old trick - catching the bit in his teeth. Well, he did that and ran away. Dan held on with his good arm until that d - d horse (excuse me, Miss Nell!) wheeled suddenly and dashed into the woods. The limbs of the trees dragged Dan out of his saddle, and his foot caught in the stirrup and Dare Devil dragged him (take some brandy, Miss Nell) until the strap broke. We picked Dan up insensible; he was delirious all night, and we thought for a time that he was done for, but, thank God! he's all right now. I hate to tell you, Miss Nell, but - you'll see how his head is - and the doctor said we mustn't let you go in if you couldn't be calm."

"I understand," I said, "I will be very careful."

And to prove how careful I could be, I broke down crying.

They didn't know what to do with me, poor fellows. They begged me not to cry, and then they said crying would do me good, and I had four pairs of broad shoulders to cry on. They were all as gentle and pitiful with me as a mother is with a baby. One of them got out his nice fresh handkerchief and wiped my eyes with it. I had come off the second time without a change of handkerchiefs, and this time without even a tooth-brush. When I had cried my trouble out and was quite calm, I told them I was ready to go to my husband. They took me to the door and I went in quietly, and seeing that he was awake, bent over him.

"I am here, Dan," I said smiling.

He tried to smile back.

"Take my head in your hands, Nell," he whispered, "and turn it so I can kiss you."

I laid my hands softly and firmly on each side of his head and turned it on the pillow. As I did so, a quantity of sand fell away.

I don't know whether his head had been properly dressed or not, but I know that for a number of days the sand fell away from it whenever I took it into my hands to turn it.

"After I fell," he told me, when he was allowed to talk, "my head was in the dirt, of course, and it was beat first against one tree and then against another. When I felt my senses leaving me, I clasped my arms tight around my head. I don't know how I managed it, but I got hold of my crippled arm with my good one, and when I was picked up my arms were locked in some way about my head. That is all that saved me."

I took the law into my own hands. Before Dan got well Dare Devil had been shot.

Chapter IV

THE REALITIES OF WAR

WHEN Dan recovered I returned to Norfolk, and there I stayed for some time, getting letters from him, taking care of uncle and developing a genius for housekeeping. One day I was out shopping when I saw everybody running toward the quay. I turned and went with the crowd. We saw the Merrimac swing out of the harbor - or did she crawl? A curious looking craft she was, that first of our ironclads, ugly and ominous.

She had not been gone many hours when the sound of guns came over the water followed by silence, terrible silence, that lasted until after the lamps were lit. Suddenly there was tumultuous cheering from the quay. The Merrimac had come home after destroying the Cumberland and the Congress.

"Well for the Congress!" we said. Her commander had eaten and drunk of Norfolk's hospitality, and then had turned his guns upon her - upon a city full of his friends. Bravely done, O Merrimac! But that night I cried myself to sleep. Under the sullen waters of Hampton Roads slept brave men and true, to whom Stars and Stripes and Southern Cross alike meant nothing now. The commander of the Congress was among the dead, and he had been my friend - I had danced with him in my father's house. Next day, the Monitor met the Merrimac and turned the tide of victory against us. Her commander was John L. Worden, who had been our guest beloved.

During all this time I had been separated from my husband. He had been detailed to make a survey of Pig Point and the surrounding country, and it was not until he reached Smithfield that he sent for me. We were beginning now to realize that war was upon us in earnest. There was the retreat from Yorktown; Norfolk was evacuated troops were moving. Everything was bustle and confusion. My husband went off with his command, the order for departure so sudden that he had not time to plan for me.

As Northern troops began to occupy the country, fearing that I would be left in the enemy's lines and so cut off from getting to him, I took the matter into my own hands and went in a covered wagon to Zuni, twenty miles distant, where I had heard that his command was encamped for a few days. After a rough ride I got there only to find that my husband had started off to Smithfield for me. We had passed each other on the road, each in a covered wagon. There was nothing to do except to wait his return that night.

As my husband's command had been ordered to join the troops at Seven Pines, I took the train for Richmond the next day, stopped a few hours, and then went to Petersburg. When I got there the Battle of Seven Pines was on. For two days it raged - for two days the booming of the cannon sounded in our ears and thundered at our hearts. Friends gathered at each other's houses and looked into each other's faces and held each other's hands, and listened for news from the field. And the sullen boom of the cannon broke in upon us, and we would start and shiver as if it had shot us, and sometimes the tears would come. But the bravest of us got so we could not weep. We only sat in silence or spoke in low voices to each other and rolled bandages and picked linen into lint. And in those two days it seemed as if we forgot how to smile.

Telegrams began to come; a woman would drop limp and white into the arms of a friend - her husband was shot. Another would sit with her hand on her heart in pallid silence until her friends, crowding around her, spoke to her, tried to arouse her, and then she would break into a cry:

"O my son! my son!"

There were some who could never be roused any more; grief had stunned and stupefied them forever, and a few there were who died of grief. One young wife, who had just lost her baby and whose husband perished in the fight, never lifted her head from her pillow. When the funeral train brought him home we laid her in old Blandford beside him, the little baby between.

Now and then when mothers and sisters were bewailing their loss and we were pressing comfort upon them, there would be a whisper, and one of us would turn to where some poor girl sat, dumb and stricken, the secret of her love for the slain wrenched from her by the hand of war. Sometimes a bereaved one would laugh!

The third day, the day after the battle, I heard that Dan was safe. Every day I had searched the columns of "Killed and Wounded" in the Richmond Despatch for his name, and had thanked God when I didn't find it. But direct news I had none until that third day. The strain had been too great; I fell ill. Owing to the general's illness at this time his staff was ordered to Petersburg, and Dan, who was engineer upon the staff, got leave to come on for a day or two in advance of the other members of it; but while I was still at death's door he was ordered off. When I at last got up, I had to be taught to walk as a child is taught, step by step; and before I was able to join my husband many battles had been fought in which he took part. I was at the breakfast-table, when, after months of weary waiting, he telegraphed me to come to Culpeper Courthouse.

This time I packed a small trunk with necessary articles, putting in heavy dresses and winter flannels. The winter does not come early in Petersburg; the weather was warm when I started, and I decided to travel in a rather light dress for the season. I did not trouble myself with hand-baggage not even a shawl. The afternoon train would put me in Richmond before night; I would stop over until morning, and that day's train would leave me in Culpeper. Just before I started, Mr. Sampson, at whose house I was staying, came in and said that an old friend of his was going to Richmond on my train and would be glad to look after me. I assented with alacrity. Before the war it was not the custom for ladies to travel alone, and, besides this, in the days of which I write traveling was attended with much confusion and many delays. I reached the depot a few minutes before train time, my escort was presented and immediately took charge of me. He was a nice-looking elderly gentleman, quite agreeable, and with just a slight odor of brandy about him. He saw me comfortably seated, and went to see after our baggage, he said. He did not return at once, but I took it for granted that he was in the smoking-car. Traveling was slower then than now. Half-way to Richmond I began to wonder what had become of my escort. But my head was too full of other things to bother very much about it. The outlook from the car window along that route is always beautiful; and then, the next day I was to see Dan. Darkness, and across the river the lights of Richmond flashed upon the view. Where was my escort? I had noticed on the train that morning a gentleman who wore the uniform of a Confederate captain and whom I knew by sight. He came up to me now.

"Excuse me, madam, but can I be of any assistance to you? I know your husband quite well."

"Do you know where my escort is?" I asked.

He looked embarrassed and tried not to smile.

"We left him at Chester, Mrs. Grey."

"At Chester? He was going to Richmond."

"Well - you see, Mrs. Grey, it was - an accident. The old gentleman got off to get a drink and the train left him."

I could not help laughing.

"If you will allow me, madam," said my new friend, "I will see you to your hotel. How about your baggage?"

"Oh!" I cried in dismay, "Mr. C has my trunk-check in his

pocket."

My new friend considered. "If he comes on the next train, perhaps that will be in time to get your trunk off with you to Culpeper. If not, your trunk will follow you immediately. I'll see the conductor and do what I can. I'm going out of town to-morrow, but Captain Jeter is here and I'll tell him about your trunkcheck. He'll be sure to see Mr. C ."

I was to see Dan the next day, and nothing else mattered. I made my mind easy about that trunk, and my new friend took me to the American, where I spent the evening very pleasantly in receiving old acquaintances and making new ones.

But with bedtime another difficulty arose: I had never slept in a room at a hotel by myself in my life. Fortunately, Mrs. Hopson, of Norfolk, happened to be spending the night there. I sent up a note asking if I might sleep with her, and went up to her room half an hour later prepared for a delightful talk about Norfolk. When we were ready for bed, she took up one of her numerous satchels and put it down on the side where I afterward lay down to sleep.

"I put that close by the bed because it contains valuables," she said with an impressive solemnity I afterward understood.

Of course I asked no questions, though she referred to the valuables several times. We were in bed and the lights had been out some time when I had occasion to ask her where she had come from there.

"Oh, Nell!" she said, "didn't you know? I've been to Charlottesville and I've come from there today. Didn't you know about it? John" (her son) "was wounded. Didn't you know about it? Of course I had to go to him. They had to perform an operation on him. I was right there when they did it." Here followed a graphic account of the operation. "It was dreadful. You see that satchel over there?" pointing to the one just beneath my head on the floor.

"Yes, I see it."

"Well, John's bones are right in there!"

"Good gracious!" I cried, and jumped over her to the

other side of the bed.

"Why, what's the matter?" she asked. "You look like you were scared, Nell. Why, Nell, the whole of John wouldn't hurt you, much less those few bones. I'm carrying them home to put them in the family buryingground. That's the reason I think so much of that satchel and keep it so close to me. I don't want John to be buried all about in different places, you see. But I don't see anything for you to be afraid of in a few bones. John's as well as ever - it isn't like he was dead, now."

I lay down quietly, ashamed of my sudden fright, but there were cold chills running down my spine.

After a little more talk she turned over, and I presently heard a comfortable snore, but I lay awake a long time, my eyes riveted on the satchel containing fragments of John. Then I began to think of seeing Dan in the morning, and fell asleep feeling how good it was that he was safe and sound, all his bones together and not scattered around like poor John's.

I reached Culpeper Courthouse the next afternoon about four o'clock. Dan met me looking tired and shabby, and as soon as he had me settled went back to camp.

"I'll come to see you as often as I can get leave," he said when he told me goodby. "We may be quartered here for some time - long enough for us to get ourselves and our horses rested up, I hope; but I'm afraid I can't see much of you. Hardly worth the trouble of your coming, is it, little woman?"

"Oh, Dan, yes," I said cheerfully; "just so you are not shot up! It would be worth the coming if I only got to see you through a car window as the train went by."

A few days after my arrival a heavy snow storm set in. As my trunk had not yet come, I was still in the same dress in which I had left Petersburg, and, though we were all willing enough to lend, clothes were so scarce that borrowing from your neighbor was a last resort. I suffered in silence for a week before my trunk arrived, and then it was exchanging one discomfort for another, for my flannels were so tight from shrinkage and so worn that I felt as if something would break every timc I moved.

During this snow-storm the roads were lined with Confederate troops marching home footsore and weary from Maryland. Long, hard marches and bloody battles had been their portion. In August they had come, after their work at Seven Pines, Cold Harbor, and Malvern Hill, to drive Pope out of Culpeper, where he was plundering. They had driven him out and pressed after, fighting incessantly. Near Culpeper there had been the battle of Cedar Mountain, where Jackson had defeated Pope and chased him to Culpeper Courthouse. Somewhat farther from Culpeper had been fought the second battle of Manassas, and, crowding upon these, the battles of Germantown, Centreville, Antietam - more than I can remember to name. Lee's army was back in Culpeper now with Federal troops at their heels, and McClellan, not Pope, in command. Civilians, women, children, and slaves feared Pope; soldiers feared McClellan - that is, as much as Lee's soldiers could fear anybody.

I found our tired army in Culpeper trying to rest and fatten a little before meeting McClellan's legions. Then - I am not historian enough to know just how it happened - McClellan's head fell and Burnside reigned in his stead. Better and worse for our army, and no worse for our women and children, for Burnside was a gentleman even as McClellan was and as Pope was not, and made no war upon women and children until the shelling of Fredericksburg.

Chapter V

I Meet Belle Boyd And See Dick In A New Light

THE tallow candles were lighted on each side of my bureau - the time came when I remembered those two tallow candles as a piece of reckless and foolish extravagance when there was a rap at my door and Mrs. Rixey entered to ask if I would share my room with a lady who had come unexpectedly. A heavy snow was falling, and the wind was blowing it into drifts. The idea of sending anybody out in such weather was not to be thought of for a moment, so saying yes I hurried through with my dressing and went down to the parlor. Mrs. Rixey's house was filled with Confederates who were there either because it was near the army or because they were awaiting an opportunity to run the blockade. Our evenings were always gay, and when I entered the parlor this evening there was as usual a merry party, and, also as usual, there were several officers of rank in the room. I was so busy sending messages to mother and Milicent by a little lady who meant to run the blockade to Baltimore as soon as possible, that I did not catch my roommate's name when Mrs. Rixey introduced her.

She seemed to be nineteen, or, perhaps twenty - rather young, I thought, to be traveling alone. True, I was not older, but then I was married, which made all the difference in the world. What made her an object of special interest to every woman present, was that she was exceedingly well dressed. I had been a long, long time since we had seen a new dress!

She was a brilliant talker, and soon everybody in the room was attracted to her, especially the men. She talked chiefly to the men - indeed, I am afraid she did not care particularly for the women - and at first we were a little piqued; but when we found that she was devoted to The Cause we were ready to forgive her anything. She soon let us know that she had come directly from Washington, where she had been a prisoner of the United States. She showed us her watch and told us how the prisoners in Washington had made the money up among themselves and presented it to her just before she left. I wish I had listened better to her account of her prison life and her adventures; but I was on the outer rim of the charmed circles, my head was full of Milicent and mother, Dan was at camp, and I couldn't see him. I got sleepy, slipped quietly out of the room, and went upstairs and to bed. My roommate undressed and got to bed so quickly that night that I did not wake. The next morning when the maid came in to make the fire, we woke up face to face in the same bed, and then she told me that her name was Belle Boyd, and I knew for the first time that my bedfellow was the South's famous female spy. When we got up she took a large bottle of cologne and poured it into the basin in which she was going to bathe. It was the first cologne I had seen for more than a year, and it was the last I saw until I ran the blockade.

That day, while we were at dinner, a servant, behind my chair, whispered:

"Somebody out dar wan' ter see you right erway, mistis - er solger."

When I went out into the hallway, there stood the most abject, pitiable-looking creature - a soldier, ragged and foot-sore! He was at the end of the hall farthest from the dining-room, and looked as if he didn't wish to attract attention.

He wore gray trousers patched with blue - or were they blue patched with gray? - and a jacket which had as much Federal blue as Confederate gray in it. From the color of his uniform, he belonged equally to both armies. His trousers were much too short for him, and altogether too small. His shoes were heavy brogans twice too large for him, and tied on with strings. He was without socks and his ankles showed naked and sore between trousers and shoes. He had on a bedticking shirt, a tobacco- bag of bedticking hung by a string from a button of shirt - a button which, by the way, was doing more than double duty - and an old slouch hat was pulled over his face.

"You wanted to see me, sir?" I asked stopping at a short distance from him.

He looked up quickly.

"How do you do, Nell?" he said. "I got leave to come from camp to see you today. My company got in from Maryland yesterday."

"Dick!" I cried in amazement; and then I burst into tears. Dick, our dandy, to look like this! Laughter mingled with weeping.

"Good gracious, Nell! what is the matter?" he said.

"Dick, Dick, how you look!"

"Hush, Nell! Good gracious! You'll have everybody in the dining-room out here to look at me."

Then I began to beg incoherently that he would go in and dine with me. I think Dick was hungry, but he was not that hungry. In his present garb starvation would not have driven him into a dining-room where ladies were. He looked toward the door with abject terror, and tried to hide himself behind the hat-rack. I was puzzled to know what I should do with him. As a young lady was my roommate it was out of the question to take him to my room, and he positively refused to go into the parlor. While we debated, the dining-room door opened and the ladies filed out into the hall. Unkempt, unshorn patched, ragged, and dirty, a very travesty of his former foppish self, Dick went through the introductions with what grace he might.

Fortunately my friends who surrounded him were in sympathy with the threadbare Confederate soldier, and ready to help him to the extent of their power. One friend, whose husband had a shirt to spare, gave that to him; another lady found him a pair of socks some one else contributed a pair of homespun drawers. I was drawn aside and consulted as to the best and most graceful way of conveying these presents to him. They feared that he might be wounded and insulted if the matter were not delicately managed. But Dick was past all that. He accepted the goods the gods provided in the spirit in which they were bestowed, and was radiant with his good luck, and with gratitude to the fair donors. While we held council he had been in Mrs. Rixey's and Miss Boyd's hands, and had had a good dinner.

As he stood in the hall ready to go back to camp, Belle Boyd came down the staircase, carrying a large new blanket shawl.

"You must let me wrap you up, lieutenant," she said, putting the shawl around Dick's shoulders and pinning it together.

Dick blushed and demurred. A shawl like that was too much - it was a princely gift, a fortune.

"I can't let you go back to camp in this thin jacket," she said, "while I have this shawl. It is serving our country, lieutenant, while it protects her soldier from the cold. I may need it? No, no, I can get others where this one came from."

There was nothing for him to do but to accept it. He looked at me with something of his old humor in his eyes as he started off.

"I'll be sure to come to see you again; Nell," he said.

After he left the house we saw him stoop, take off his shoes, and walk off with them in his hands. His feet left marks of blood in the snow. Shoes had been dealt out to the army only that morning, and his feet were so sore that his heavy, ill-fitting brogans were unendurable.

I have heard of many generous deeds like this done by Belle Boyd. Once, when riding out to review some troops near Winchester, she met a soldier, a mere boy, trudging along painfully on his bare feet. She took off her own shoes and made him put them on; they were fine cloth gaiters laced at the side, and trimmed with patent leather. Some one remonstrated; the shoes would not last the boy long enough to pay for her sacrifice.

"Oh," she said, "if it rests his poor young feet only a little while, I am repaid. He is not old enough to be away from his mother."

She did not spend another night with us. She seemed to feel that she had the weight of the Confederacy on her shoulders, and took the afternoon train for Richmond.

Chapter VI

A Faithful Slave And A Hospital Ward

Not long after this I had to give up my room to Governor Bailey of Florida and his family. They had come on in search of their son, whom they had for months believed to be dead, and who, they had only recently learned, was alive and in the mountains near Culpeper Court-house.

It seems that young Bailey had been shot at the battle of Cedar Mountain and left on the field for dead. An old negro, his bodyservant, had carried him off by stealth to a hut in the woods, and there, with such simple resources as he had, had dressed and bandaged the wound. The hut was a mere shell of a house, a habitation for bats and owls; it had been unused so long that no paths led to it, and Uncle Reuben's chief object in carrying his master there was to hide him from the Yankees. He had no medicine, no doctor, no help, the master was ill for a long time from his wounds and with a slow fever, and through it all Uncle Reuben never left him except at night to forage for both. Food in the Confederacy was far from plentiful, and under the circumstances almost impossible to get. The hardships they endured seem inconceivable today. Afraid to show himself lest in doing so he should turn his master over into the hands of the dreaded Yankees, the faithful old servant saw no way of communicating with the family. He was in a strange country; he could not leave his charge, alone and desperately ill, long enough to seek advice and assistance, and, besides, how was he to know the friend who would help him from the man who might betray him? He knew but one token - the Confederate uniform, and that was not always to be trusted, for spies wore it.

Confederate troops must have passed near his hiding-place several times, but in his anxiety to save his master from the Federals, the negro hid him from the Confederates as well.

It happened at last that a party of skirmishers who had frequently deployed along the obscure roads intersecting the country, noticed, rising from the depths of the forest, a thin streak of smoke suggesting deserters or spies, and began to investigate. So, it happened that they came upon the hut, and a poor, old, half- starved negro watching what seemed to be little more than a human skeleton. When convinced that his discoverers were really Confederates, his joy and eagerness knew no bounds.

"Ef any uv you gentlemen will jes send a 'spatch to Ole Marster," he said tremulously, "Ole Marster'll be hyer toreckly. He'll be hyer jes ez quick ez de kyars kin git him hyer. We ain't got no money. But Ole Marster'll pay fur de 'spatch jes ez soon ez he comes. Ole Marster's rich. He'll pay fur anything anybody do fur Mars Hugh, an' be thankful ter do it. Ole Marster'll come arter Mars Hugh jes ez quick ez I kin git him word. He'll pay anybody fur evvything."

The soldiers hardly knew what to do; perhaps they never considered that they could do anything but what they did: ride away and leave behind them the pair in the hut. Perhaps, poor fellows, there was nothing else they could do. Comfortable hospitals for Southern soldiers were scarce, and the Confederate soldier had little to give to any one, even to his sick comrade.

The negro, the guardian in this instance was not anxious to have his charge moved. His whole concern was "to git word to Ole Marster."

"I kin take kyeer uv him," he insisted "jes lak I bin doin' 'twell Ole Marster come. Den he'll know what to do. Mars

Hugh ain't fitten to move now. Ef twarn't don jes right, he couldn't stan' it, case he's too weakly. 'Twon't do fur no strange folks to tech him nor 'sturb him, lessen dey know how. Mars Hugh jes same ez er baby."

They gave the negro the rations they had with them, and the whisky in their canteens - it was all they had to give except their scant clothes - and rode on to Culpeper Court house, where one of them sent the despatch to "Ole Marster," according to the directions Uncle Reuben had given. And our Florida party was "Ole Marster" and his wife, and poor Hugh Bailey's young wife and her uncle.

It was well into the night after their arrival when four soldiers carried up to my room a stretcher holding a skeleton of a man. A gaunt, ragged old negro followed.

The next day the party started for home, but they never got poor Hugh as far as Florida. They stopped in Richmond at the Exchange, and there Hugh Bailey died the next day.

And now began for me the nursing in hospital wards that made up so large a part of our lives during the war.

"Jeter shot, perhaps fatally. Go to the hospital and see what you can do for him. I have telegraphed to his wife and mother. "DAN."

The orderly who brought me this message from my husband said that Captain Jeter's command had been in a skirmish that day, and that the captain had fallen, mortally wounded, it was thought.

I went to him at once. He was lying unconscious across the bed as if he had fallen or been dropped there, dressed in full uniform with his coat buttoned up to his throat, breathing stertorously, and moaning. There was a small black hole in his temple. I thought he must be uncomfortable with his clothes on, and proposed to the nurse that we should try to undress him, but she said he was dying and it would only disturb him. All that day and until late that night I stayed with him, changing the towels on his head, wiping the ooze from his lips, listening to that agonizing moaning, and thinking of the wife and mother who could not reach him. About ten o'clock he seemed to be strangling.

"It's phlegm in his throat," the nurse said. She ran her finger down his throat, pulling out a quid of tobacco that had been in his mouth when he was shot and that had lain there ever since.

He died at midnight, and his mother came the next day at noon. I don't know which was the hardest to stand, her first burst of agony or her endless questions when she could talk.

"Did he suffer much, Nell?"

"Not much, I think. He was unconscious from the time he was shot."

"Nell, did he send me any message? Did he call for me?"

"He was unconscious," I repeated gently, "and we must be thankful that he was. If he had been conscious he would have suffered more."

"Yes, yes; I reckon I am thankful. I don't know how I am now. But I'm trying to submit myself to the will of the Lord. Nellie, you don't know what a sweet baby he was! the prettiest little fellow! as soon as he could walk, he was always toddling after me and pulling at my skirts."

I turned my head away.

"Last night I dozed for a minute and I dreamed about him. He was my baby again, and I had him safe in my arms, and there never had been any war. But I didn't sleep much. I couldn't come as soon as I got the telegram. I had to wait for a train. And I was up nearly all night cooking things to bring him."

She opened her basket and satchel and showed me. They were full of little cakes and crackers, wine jellies and blancmange, and other delicacies for the sick.

"Do you think if I had gotten here in time he could have eaten them?" she asked wistfully.

"He could not eat anything," I sail choking back my tears.

"You don't think he was hungry at all Nell? The soldiers have so little to eat some times - and I have heard it said that people are sometimes hungry when they are dying."

"Dear Mrs. Jeter, he looked well and strong except for the wound. You know the troops had just returned from the valley where they had plenty to eat."

"I am glad of that. I was just getting a box ready to send him full of everything I thought he would like. And I had some clothes for him. I began making the clothes as soon as I heard the troops had come back to Culpeper. You say he was wounded in the head?"

Neither of us closed our eyes that night. She walked the floor asking the same questions over and over again, and I got so I answered yes or no just as I saw she wanted yes or no and without regard to the truth.

Several months after this I saw Captain Jeter's widow. She was surrounded by his little children - none of them old enough to realize their loss.

"Nell," she said, "you remember the day in Petersburg when we stood together and watched the troops start off for Norfolk - and everybody was cheering?"

"Yes."

"Well, war does not look to me now as it did then. God grant it may spare your husband to you, Nell!"

I shivered.

I called on another widowed friend. Her husband - a captain, too - had been sent home, his face mutilated past recognition by the shell that killed him. Her little ones were around her, and the captain's sword was hanging on the wall. When I spoke to her of it as a proud possession, her eyes filled. His little boy said with flashing eyes:

"It's my papa's s'ode. I wants to be a man. An' I'll take it down and kill all the Yankees!"

"H-sh!" his mother put her hand over his mouth. "God grant there may be no war when you are a man!" she said fervently.

"Amen!" I responded.

"Oh, Nell," she said, "when it's all over, what good will it do? It will just show that one side could fight better than the other, or had more money and men than the other. It won't show that anybody's right. You can't know how it is until it hits you, Nell I'm proud of him, and proud of his sword; I wouldn't have had him out of it all. I wouldn't have had him a coward. But oh, Nell, I feel that war is wrong! I'm sorry for every Northern woman who has a circle like this around her, and a sword like that hanging on her wall."

The little boy put his arm around her neck. "Mamma," he said, "are you sorry for the Yankees?"

"My dear," she said, "I am sorry for all little boys who haven't got a papa, and I'm sorry for their mammas. And I don't want you ever to kill anybody."

Chapter VII

TRAVELING THROUGH DIXIE IN WAR TIMES

OUR troops had to get out of winter quarters before they were well settled in them. I am not historian enough to explain how it was, but the old familiar trip "On to Richmond" had been started again, Burnside directing it. Every new Federal commander-in-chief started for Richmond as soon as he was in command. There was a popular song called "Richmond is a Hard Road to Travel." They always found it so, though they got there eventually.

The cavalry, as usual, were on the wing first. General Rooney (W. H. F.) Lee's division was sent to Fredericksburg in November, I think. My husband, of course, went with it. I was to go to Richmond and wait until I heard whether it would be safe for me to join him.

From Richmond I ran over to Petersburg, saw many old friends and ran back to Richmond again, fearful lest a message should come from Dan and I should miss it, I looked for a telegram every day, and kept my trunk packed. It was well that I did.

One morning my door was burst open unceremoniously and Dan rushed in.

"Ready to go, Nell?"

"Yes."

"Come. Now."

I put on my bonnet, caught up my satchel, stuffed brush, tooth-brush, and comb into it and was ready. Dan had stepped into the hall to call a porter to take the trunk down. We followed it, jumped into the omnibus, and it rolled off - all this in about five minutes from the time he burst my door open. On the omnibus, among other passengers, was a gentleman who had a brother in Dan's command. This gentleman had so many questions to ask about the army, and so many messages to send his brother that Dan and I hardly exchanged a dozen sentence before we were at the depot. He established me in my seat, got my baggage checked, sat down, and then exclaiming:

"Good gracious! I forgot that bundle for General Lee. It's on top of the omnibus, Nell. I'll be back in a minute," and darted off.

At the next station, when the conductor came for my ticket, I said:

"See my husband, please. He must be in the smoking-car."

A gentleman across the aisle remarked:

"Excuse me, madam, but I think the gentleman who came in with you got left. I saw him get off the omnibus with a bundle in his hand and run after the car, but he missed it."

"Then I don't know what to do," I said in despair to the conductor. "I haven't a ticket, and I haven't any money."

"Where are you going?" he asked kindly.

"I don't know!" I gasped.

The conductor looked blank. I explained the manner of my starting to him.

"Do you know where your husband's command is stationed?"

"No, I don't know that either. You see," I explained, "as he belongs to the cavalry it is much harder to keep up with his whereabouts than if he were in the infantry."

"What division is he in?"

"General Rooney Lee's."

"Do you know what brigade?"

"Chambliss's."

"All right. I know what to do with you, then. You stop at Milford. Your husband will come on the freight this afternoon - at least, that's what I expect him to do. Your best plan is to wait at Milford for him."

When we reached Milford the conductor took me out and introduced me to the landlord of the tavern, and I was shown into what I suppose might be called by grace the reception-room. It was literally on the ground floor, being built on native brown earth. The ceiling was low, the room was full of smoke, and rough-looking men sat about with pipes in their mouths. I asked for a private room, and was shown into one upstairs, but this was so cold that I went out into the porch which overhung the street and walked up and down in the sun to keep myself warm. Very soon the gong sounded for dinner. I went down, sat with a rough crowd around a long table, swallowed what I could, and went back to my promenade on the porch. After a time an ambulance drove up and stopped under the porch, and an orderly sang out:

"Adjutant of the Thirteenth here?"

I leaned over the railing.

"I am his wife," I said.

He saluted. "Can you tell me where the adjutant is, ma'am?"

"He will be here on the next train."

"That might be midnight, ma'am, or it might be to-morrow. My orders were to meet the adjutant here about this time."

"The adjutant got left by the regular passenger. But a freight was to leave Richmond soon after the passenger, and the adjutant will come on that."

"The freight?" the orderly looked doubtful. "Maybe so."

"What do you mean?" I asked.

"Well, ma'am, all trains are uncertain, and freight trains more so. And sometimes freight trains are mighty pertickular about what kind of freight they carry."

I laughed, but the orderly did not see the point. Dan's

body-servant was to drive the ambulance back, so the orderly, turning it over to a man whom he picked up in the tavern, went back to camp according to instructions. As soon as he was out of sight I began to repent. If Dan shouldn't come on that freight, what would I do with myself and that strange man and the ambulance and the mules? It was getting late when the welcome sound of a whistle broke upon my ear and the freight came creeping in. On the engine beside the engineer stood my husband, with that abominable little bundle of General Lee's in his hand.

"Josh got left somewhere," Dan said of his servant, "the man will have to drive."

At last we were off, Dan and I sitting comfortably back in the ambulance. I was very cold when I first got in, but he wrapped me up well in the blanket and I snuggled up against him, and began to tell him how nice and warm he was, and how thankful I was that there was no possibility of his getting left from me between here and camp.

"I had a time of it to come on that freight," he said.

"The orderly said you would." I repeated the orderly's remark, and Dan laughed.

"He told the truth. I had to do more swearing to the square inch than I have been called upon to do for some time. I knew you didn't even know where you were going, and that I must get here to-night. As soon as I heard about the freight, I went to the conductor. He said passengers couldn't be taken on the freight, it was against orders. 'I belong to the army as you see,' I urged, 'I am an officer and it is important for me to rejoin my command.' He insisted still that I couldn't go, that it was against orders. I told him that it was a bundle for General Lee that had got me left, and I pictured your predicament in moving colors. He was obdurate. 'If the freights begin to take passengers,' he said, 'there would soon be no room for any other sort of freight on them.' I felt like kicking him. It was then that I told him that orders were not made for fools to carry out, and the swearing began. I threatened to report him.

He looked uneasy and was ready to make concessions which politeness had not been able to win, but I walked off. Evidently, like a mule, he respected me more for cursing him. I had my plan laid. Just as the train moved out of the station I swung on to the engine, and politely introduced myself to the engineer. He had overheard my conversation with the conductor - the first part of it, not the part where the swearing came in - and he invited me to get off the engine. While we were debating the engine was traveling. I saw that he was about to stop it.

"Quick as a flash I had my pistol at his head.

"'Now,' I said, 'drive on with this engine, or I'll kill you and run it myself!' I am not telling you all the words I used, Nell, you'll forgive me this time, I had to get to you, and honest English is wasted on fools and mules. 'Hold off!' he said, 'and don't put that d - d thing so close to my head, and you can ride up here and be d - d to you.' The invitation was not very polite, but I accepted it. I gave him some good tobacco, and we got to be friends before I got off."

The short day was done. I was tired and warm and sleepy and went to sleep while Dan was talking. I don't know how long I had dozed when the driver doubled up suddenly and turned head over heels backward into my lap. I struggled from under him, and Dan gave him a push that helped to free me and at the same time jumped on to the driver's seat and caught up the lines.

"Lord-a-mussy on me!" I heard the man groaning, "dat ar d - n mu-el! she have kicked me in de pit er my stummick!"

He gathered himself together in a corner of the ambulance, and continued to express forcible opinions of the mule.

"Dan," I said, "please get away from there! That mule might kick you."

"Don't be silly, Nell! Somebody's got to drive."

"But, Dan, if you get kicked, you can't drive."

"I won't get kicked. I know how to talk to a mule. Just shut your ears, Nell, if you don't want to hear me. I've got to convince this mule. She's just like that engineer and conductor. As soon as I get through giving her my opinion in language she can understand, she'll travel all right."

Presently Dan called out: "You can unstop your ears now, Nell - I think she understands."

"Dan," I said, "are you cold out there?"

"Not a bit of it! This isn't anything to a soldier. But a soldier's wife, eh, Nell? Getting to be rather hard lines, isn't it?"

"Dan," I said, my teeth chattering "don't it seem that I have had more adventures in one day than I am entitled to?"

"Rather! By the way, Josh got on that same freight. How he managed it, the Lord only knows! Worked himself in with the brakeman, I suppose. But he got off - to look around, I reckon just like him! - at some station before Milford and got left. He'll come straggling into camp to-morrow. You see there's another accident you can credit your account with. Josh could have driven these mules instead of that fool white man over there who don't know what to do with a mule. Then I would have been back there entertaining you, and you would have been complimenting me by going to sleep." He drove on singing:

"Sweet Nellie is by my side!" We caught up with another ambulance. In it were an army friend of Dan's and his wife, and she proved the straw that broke the back of my endurance. She played the martyr. She had rugs, and shawls, and blankets. I cross-examined her and made her show that she hadn't been left on a car by herself without a ticket or a cent of money, and with no knowledge of where she was going, that the driver of her ambulance hadn't been kicked in the stomach and tumbled himself backward into her lap and nearly broken her bones, and that my case was far worse than hers. But in spite of it, she complained of everything, and had Dan and her husband sympathizing so with her that they had no time to sympathize with me. I sat, almost frozen, huddled up in the one shawl that answered for shawl, blanket, and rug, and tried to keep my teeth from chattering and myself from hating that whining Mrs. Gummidge of a woman.

At last our ambulance drew up in front of the Rev. Mr. McGuire's, where we were to stop There was a hot supper ready, in parlor and dining-room cheerful flames leaped up from hickory logs on bright brass fire-dogs, and our welcome was as cheery as the glow of the fire. As our ambulance had driven into the gate a few minutes in advance of the other, and as Dan had also engaged board for me several days before, I had a right to the first choice of rooms. One of these was large with a bright fire burning in the fireplace, and a great downy feather-bed on the four-poster; the other was small, and had neither fireplace nor feather-bed. Of course "Mrs. Gummidge" got the best room. Dan had to go back to camp. I slept on my hard bed in my cold room and cried for Milicent and mother; and the next morning I broke the ice in my bowl when I went to take my bath. I was very, very miserable that morning. I was not out of my twenties, I had been a spoiled child, I had not seen Milicent or mother since my marriage, I had nearly lost my husband, and I had been ill unto death. Following my husband around as I did, I yet saw very little of him, and I endured hardships of every sort. I was in the land of war, and in spite of all his efforts to protect me life was full of fears and horrors.

I do not mean that it was all woe. There were smiles, and music, and laughter, too; my hosts were kind, Dan came over from camp whenever he could, and life was too full of excitement ever to be dull. During the day I managed fairly well - it was at night that the horrors overwhelmed me. My room was cheerless, my bed was hard and cold - I wanted Milicent, I wanted mother. I felt that the time had come when I must see them and I couldn't: there was no way! The longing grew upon me the more I struggled against it, until there was no risk I would not have run to see them. I was sitting in the parlor one night thinking with indescribable longing of the happy, care-free days in Norfolk, and seeing dissolving pictures of home in the hickory fire. Tears were rolling down my cheeks, for while I was living over those dear old days I was living in the present, too. Suddenly I heard a voice in the hall - Dan's and another's!

I sprang up. And there was Dan, and behind him in the doorway stood a graceful figure in a long wrap. And a face - Milicent's face - pale and weary, but indescribably lovely and loving, was looking toward me with shining eyes.

"Millie!"

"Nell!"

That was one time I forgot Dan, but he didn't mind. He stayed with us as long as he could, and after he left Milicent and I talked and talked. Milicent - she was a widow now - had come all the way from Baltimore to see me - she had left mother and Bobby to come to see me! My little bed wasn't hard any more, my room wasn't cheerless any more; I didn't mind having to break the ice for my bath. Ah, me, what a night that was and how happy we were until Dan's command was moved!

Millie and I - Catholics - wish to pay tribute to the sweet piety of that Protestant home which sheltered us. Every evening the big Bible was brought out and prayers were held, the negro servants coming in to share in the family devotions.

Chapter VIII

BY FLAG OF TRUCE

Milicent tells how she got from Baltimore to Dixie.

THE War Department of the United States issued a notice that on such a date a flag-of- truce boat would go from Washington to Richmond, and that all persons wishing to go must obtain passes and come to that city by a certain date.

I had not heard from my sister, Mrs. Grey, for some time. We were very anxious about her, and I determined to seize this opportunity to get to her.

I was fortunate in making one of a party of three ladies, one of whom was Mrs. Montmorency, the widow of an English officer, and the other Mrs. Dangerfield, of Alexandria, Virginia. On our arrival at Washington late at night, we found all the hotels crowded and were told that it would be impossible to get a room anywhere. Fortunately for us, Mrs. Dangerfield was acquainted with the proprietor of one of the hotels where we inquired, and here, after much difficulty, we secured two small rooms As he left us the old lady said triumphantly:

"Now, see what's in a name! If my name hadn't been Dangerfield none of us could have gotten a place to sleep in to-night."

The next morning we started for the flag-of- truce boat. Immediately upon our arrival our baggage was weighed and all over two hundred pounds refused transportation. The confusion was indescribable. As soon as the steamer cleared the wharf every stateroom was locked, and the five hundred passengers on board, with the exception of the children, were subjected to a rigid examination - their persons, their clothing, their trunks were all thoroughly searched. We were marched down two by two between guards, and passed into the lower cabin, where four women removed and searched our clothing; our shoes, stockings, and even our hair were subjected to rigid inspection.

Mrs. Dangerfield being the oldest lady on board was by courtesy exempted. As for myself, I fell into the hands of a pleasant woman, who looked ashamed of the office she had to perform. She passed her hand lightly over and within my dress, and over my hair; touched my pockets and satchels, which I willingly showed her, and dismissed me with a smile and the kind remark, "Oh, I know you have nothing contraband," while around me stood ladies shivering in one garment.

I had tea and sugar, both contraband articles, in a large satchel upstairs in the care of the provost marshal. I out-Yankeed the Yankees this trip. As soon as I had heard that we were to be searched and have our things taken from us, I had walked up to the provost marshal, told him I had tea and coffee - a small quantity of each - and asked to be allowed to use them. In the gruffest manner he bade me bring them immediately to him. My dejected looks must have inspired him with some pity, for when I went off and brought back my satchel and handed it to him, he turned and said in the kindest manner:

"Now I have saved them for you. After the search is over come to me and I will return them to you."

I thanked him and hurried off to impart the good news to my friend Mrs. Dangerfield. I found her in a most animated discussion with an officer who had just pronounced her camphor-bottle contraband. The old lady was asserting loudly her inability to stand the trip or to live without her camphor-bottle. After much argument and persuasion she was allowed to retain it.

The scenes on deck at this time were too painful to dwell upon. Mothers who had periled everything and spent their last dollar in buying shoes for their children had to see them rudely taken away. Materials for clothing, and pins, needles, buttons, thread, and all the little articles so needful at home and so difficult to obtain in the Confederacy at that time were pronounced contraband. Men went about with their arms filled with plunder taken from defenseless women who stood wringing their hands and pleading, crying, arguing, quarreling.

By this time we were far down the Potomac. Weak, hungry, and seasick, we were glad when dinner-time drew near. The official notice had stated that food would be provided, which we, of course, had construed into three meals a day of good steamboat fare. The bell rang out loudly at last, and we all rushed to the cabin, where to our utter consternation we saw nothing whatever to eat, no set table, and nothing that looked like eating. Coming up the steps was a dirty boathand with a still dirtier bucket and a string of tin cups. He deposited these on a table and then called upon the ladies to help themselves to atrocious coffee, without milk, sugar, or spoons. Down he went again, and came up laden with tin plates piled one on the other, and containing what he called a sandwich. This sandwich was a chunk - not a slice - of bread, spread with dreadful mustard, a piece of coarse ham and another chunk of bread. Each person was generously allowed one of the tin plates and one sandwich. The very thought of swallowing such food was revolting, and more particularly so because we were tantalized with odors of beefsteak and chicken and other appetizing delicacies prepared for the officers' table.

How thankful I was to the provost for confiscating my tea and coffee and sugar and crackers and ginger-cakes! Each of our party had something to add. Down upon the lower deck we had seen an immense pile of loaves of bread, and near them a large stove. We coaxed the sailor in charge to get us a clean loaf from the center of the pile and to put our tea on his stove to draw. In a few moments we disappeared to enjoy in our stateroom the luxury of a cup of tea! How others fared I do not know. We were the only people, I think, who had saved any tea. Almost every one had brought a few crackers, or cakes of some kind which they had managed to keep, and these they must have lived on with the abominable coffee.

When we reached the boat that morning only one stateroom was vacant, and this we contrived to secure. It was crowded comfort for three persons, but we were thankful. When night came our less fortunate fellow travelers were scattered in every direction on the floor, their only accommodations filthy camp mattresses without sheets, pillows, or covering of any kind except their own cloaks and shawls.

We traveled slowly and cautiously, fearing that in the night our flag might not be distinctly seen and we might be fired upon. The provost and his officers were in most things polite and kind. The men got up a little play between decks for the amusement of the ladies; but our party was too ultra-Southern even to look on.

We remained off Fortress Monroe all night, only starting at daylight for the James River. The trip up the James was accomplished in safety and without incident of special interest, if we except a very sudden and desperate love affair between a Southern girl and a Federal officer and the amusement which it afforded us.

As our boat neared the wharf at City Point, on all sides were heard cries of:

"Here we are in Dixie!"

As soon as we were landed a rush was made for the cars, and after everybody was seated the provost marshal came through bidding us good- by, shaking hands with many and kissing the pretty young girls. He had been very kind, and, as far as lay in his power, had done so much for the comfort of all and for the pleasure of the young people that most of us felt as if we were parting from a friend. Indeed, some were so enthusiastic that before we reached City Point they went among the passengers begging subscriptions to a fund for purchasing the provost a handsome diamond ring as a testimonial. Many, however, refused indignantly, declaring that they did not feel called upon to reward the provost for confiscating every article possible, and for giving us for seven consecutive meals spoiled bacon, mustard, and undrinkable coffee.

In Petersburg little or no preparation had been made for us although the hotel proprietors knew the truce boat was expected that afternoon at City Point. We were scarcely able to secure an ordinary supper, and had to sleep, eight or ten in a room, on mattresses laid on the floor, and which, though clean and comfortable enough, were without covering. The next day we parted to go in different directions.

Chapter IX

I Make Up My Mind To Run The Blockade

LATE one day we saw an ambulance driving up to the gate through the pouring rain. A few minutes after, Patsy, the housemaid, came in to say that the adjutant had sent for his wife and her sister. We supposed that the two men with the ambulance were rough and common soldiers - one of them, in fact, the one who had given the message to Patsy, was a negro driver - and sent them around to the kitchen to warm and dry themselves. Very soon Aunt Caroline, the cook and a great authority, came in hurriedly and attacked Mrs. McGuire.

"Law, mistess! Y'all sholy orter ax one er dem men in de house. He sholy orten ter bin sont to de kitchen. He ain't got no bizness in de kitchen. He's quality. You orter ax him to come to de parlor. He specks you gwine ter ax him to come to de parlor, case he done bresh hissef up, and he's puttin' sweet grease on his har, and he say he kin play on de orgin."

Such accomplishments as these changed the whole situation. Aunt Caroline was sent to fetch him. When she threw open the door and announced him and he entered, bowing low and gracefully, we could hardly restrain a laugh, for we had a good view of the top of his head, and it was fairly ashine! He was Lieutenant Dimitri of New Orleans, my husband's courier, who had been sent as our escort. A most efficient and agreeable one he proved.

If I had only been a young lady following my father or brother around, how interesting these memoirs might be made, for Lieutenant Dimitri was only one of many charming men I met. Available heroes pass through, bow, and make their exits. And I am afraid of boring my friends with the one hero who remains because he is my husband; consequently I keep him as modestly as possible in the background. He had risen steadily in rank, and I was proud of him, but I must say that my memory is less vivid as to his deeds of gallantry than it is to what might have been reckoned minor matters by an older woman. The greatest crosses of my life were separation from my mother and sister, telling my husband good-by, and beholding him in a hopelessly shabby uniform. The greatest blessings of my life were found in the little courtesies and kindnesses of life and in getting my husband back to me, safe and sound.

When morning came it was still raining, and the roads in such a condition that Mr. McGuire, fearing our ambulance would break down, opposed our going. But I knew that the men and team must return to camp according to orders, so we started off in spite of the weather and Mr. McGuire's protest.

We had not gone far when our driver was halted by a vidette who barred the way.

"Is Adjutant Grey's wife in the ambulance?"

"Yessuh."

"Turn back. Smallpox ahead."

The driver turned another road. It was only a short distance before we were halted again.

"Adjutant Grey's wife in the ambulance?"

"Yessuh, she sho is."

"Turn around. Smallpox this way."

"Lord! how is I ter go?" groaned the driver.

At the next fork the driver paused with a look of utter distraction.

"I don't kyeer whicherway we go, dar'll be smallpox in de road sayin' we can't go datter way." And he drove recklessly on the way the mules seemed to prefer. The mules struck it.

A vidette halted us again, but it was to say that we were

traveling in the right direction and to give minute directions for the rest of our journey. There was a village and its neighborhood to be avoided, and we had to make a wide detour before the driver put us down, according to orders, at Mr. Wright's.

Dan came in quite soon, looking as shabby as one of his own orderlies, but glad enough to see me. For some time here I was in a fool's paradise in spite of the war and the fact that mother was far away in Baltimore, ignorant of what might be happening to us, for camp was very near, there were no active hostilities, and Dan came to see me every day.

Then the cavalry received marching orders. The night after I heard it I determined to tell Dan of a decision I had come to. Milicent had not spoken, but I knew the drift of her thoughts and purposes. We had not heard once from mother and Bobby since she left them in Baltimore. Milicent was going to them, and I had made up my mind to go with her. There was no return to Baltimore by flag of truce; the only way to get there was to run the blockade, a most dangerous and doubtful undertaking at this period of the war. But Milicent's boy was in Baltimore, and mother was there. She had come to me; she would go to them, and I intended to go with her.

My heart was set on seeing mother. To be left alone now by both Milicent and Dan would drive me crazy; for Milicent to run the blockade alone would serve me as ill. Besides, I wanted some things for myself; some pins and needles, and nice shoes and pocket handkerchiefs and a new hat and a new cloak, and I wanted a new uniform for Dan. Dan had had no new uniform since his first promotion, a long time ago. He was an officer of high rank, and he was still wearing his old private's uniform. He had traveled through rain and snow and mud, and had slept on the ground and fought battles in it. Though I had many times cleaned that uniform, darned it, patched it, turned it, scoured it, done everything that was possible to rejuvenate it, my shabby-looking soldier was a continual reproach to me. When Dan would come to see me I used to make him wrap up in a sheet or blanket while I worked away on his clothes with needle and thread, soap and water and smoothing irons. I was ready to run the blockade for a new uniform for Dan if for nothing else, but to tell him that I was going to run the blockade - there was the rub! Evening came and Dan with it and the telling had to be done somehow.

"Dan," I began, patting the various patches on his shabby knee, "I want you to have a new uniform."

"Wish me a harp and a crown, Nell!

One's about as easy as the other. You'll have to take it out in wanting, my girl."

"I expect I could buy Confederate cloth in Baltimore."

"Maybe - if you were there."

"Dan, I think I'll slip across the border and buy you a Confederate uniform, gold lace and all, from a Yankee tradesman, and then slip back here with it, and behold you in all the glory of it. Wouldn't that be nice, Dan?"

"Rather!"

Dan took in his patches at a glance, perhaps by way of mental comparison between himself in this and himself in the imaginary new uniform. But I saw he did not understand me at all - I had to make things plain.

"Dan," I said, "I am going to Baltimore."

"What?" he thundered.

"I am going to run the blockade with Millie."

"Have you lost your senses?"

"No, Dan. But I'm going to run the blockade with Millie - to get you a new uniform."

"Nell, don't be a goose!"

"And some shirts and some socks and some pins and needles - and I want to see mother - and Bobby - and - I'm going."

"I'm not going to allow you to attempt such a thing!" he said gravely.

"I want to see mother - and to get a new uniform - and other things."

Dan looked at me as if he thought I was crazy.

"Milicent is going - and I think I ought to go with her."

"I don't want Millie to go - I don't think she ought to try it; and I won't permit you to go off on such a wild-goose chase."

I was silent a minute, trying to think how to tell him as respectfully as I could that I differed with him on this point. It all ended by my repeating in a stupid, poll-parrot fashion:

"I'm going with Millie to Baltimore."

Dan looked at me as if he would like to spank me! Here was his obedient, docile girl- bride blossomed into a contumacious, rebellious wife!

I was ready to cry - nay, I was crying - but I still affirmed that I must go to Baltimore. Dan reasoned and argued, but that didn't do any good. Then he swore, but swearing didn't alter the case. The case was, indeed, beyond Dan, but he made a long and hard fight, and didn't surrender for a long while. I cried all night, and he reasoned all night. When he saw that the case was hopeless, he started us to Petersburg under suitable escort. We had to go first to Petersburg in order to get the money which we wished to take North to exchange for all the goods and chattels we might be able to smuggle South.

Dan detailed a driver and an ambulance for our service and Lieutenant Johnston to act as escort. The morning we started it looked cloudy. Dan tried to dissuade us. I said I had always been a good weather prophet and I didn't think it would rain. Millie reinforced me.

But when it actually came to telling Dan good-by, I broke down. His threadbare clothes plead with me both ways. I hung around his neck and did so much crying that he got sorry for me and helped me off.

"When I get you a new uniform, Dan -" I sobbed, as he tucked the old blanket shawl about me where I sat in the ambulance.

"Uniform be!" growled Dan. Then, seeing, my crestfallen look, "I reckon I'll like it well enough, Nell - when it comes. Good-by, girls. You're mighty big geese God bless you! If you change your minds in Petersburg - but, Lord! an earthquake wouldn't change you! Good-by, my darling - God bless you! I reckon you'll get along all right."

The rusty coat-sleeve was out of sight, and I was on my way.

Chapter X

I Cross The Country In An Ambulance And The Pamunkey On A Lighter

As we traveled along farther and farther from Dan, I kept on crying softly to myself now and then, turning my face from Milicent. Presently her arm stole around me.

"Do you feel so badly, darling?"

"I hate to leave Dan - I can't bear it!"

"Then we'll turn back, Nell."

And our astonished driver and escort received orders to turn back toward camp.

"But in a few days," I sobbed, "Dan- will-be-gone. And you-will be-gone. And I can't stand that!"

And to the further confusion of escort driver, and mules, we were turned again.

"Better not to do dat too often, lessen we won't git nowhar!" our driver muttered to himself. "Dese mules is clean upsot in dar rnin's."

I was upset in my mind, too. I continued to cry in a helpless, hopeless fashion, and was feeling that nothing on earth could make me more wretched than I already was when it began raining. Lieutenant Johnston, who had the soul of Mark Tapley, prophesied a shower and refused to leave his seat with the driver, but in a little while he was driven inside with us. It rained harder and harder - it poured. The ambulance began to leak and the straw on the floor got wet. Milicent and I huddled together under the old blanket shawl and drew over that a ragged piece of oilcloth; but the rain soaked through. Where Lieutenant Johnston sat there was a steady dripping, bursting now and then into a stream. But he was not to be daunted by discomforts or difficulties. He invented a trough for carrying off the water by making a dent in his broad-brimmed hat, pulling the brim into a point, and sticking it through a rent in the ambulance cover; and he was so merry over it all, and so convinced that things might be far worse and would soon be much better, that we were beginning to laugh at our own expense, when a sullen rushing and roaring reminded us that the worst of our troubles were still before us. We looked out of our ambulance upon the swollen waters of the Pamunkey River.

The thing on which we were to cross it was moored to the bank by a great chain. It was a lighter crowded with men and horses. There were soldiers at the ends and sides holding long sticks which they used as poles to direct and govern the craft. Our ambulance and mules were driven on along with other teams, and we walked into the midst of rearing and plunging horses, that threatened every minute to back off the lighter into the river and drag us with them, while our craft was making its slow way to the opposite bank.

I stood between two horses that reared and plunged the whole time. The men who held them had hard work to control them and, I must add, that they swore roundly, and confess that this was the one occasion of my life when I did not undervalue that accomplishment or wish to put any restraint upon its free exercise. The truth is I was so scared that I was ready to help along with either the work or the swearing, if I had only known how.

As one of the men was trying his best to keep the horse he was holding from plunging and kicking itself into the river, or plunging and kicking itself on me, he caught my eye in the middle of an oath, and interrupted himself to begin an apology. The horse took advantage of this to make more vigorous demonstrations.

"Oh! oh!" I cried in terror, "finish - finish what you were saying to the horse! He's going to jump on me, and I'll have to say it myself if you don't!"

I didn't realize what I was saying until I heard a chuckle from the men within hearing distance. They knew that I was beside myself with terror, and did their best to smother their laughter. But I was past caring for public opinion. I was in an agony of terror. There was no other place for me to stand-horses, kicking, plunging, rearing horses were crowded everywhere. A lighter is the rudest excuse for a boat. Ours was made of planks crossed and nailed together, and between their wide spaces, just under my feet, I saw the swollen waters, upon which we seemed to be tossed, and careened, and whipped about without the control or guidance of those on board. Never before or since, never during any period of the war, was I in such a state of helpless fright as on that day when I crossed the mad Pamunkey on a lighter with swearing men and kicking horses around me and the water bubbling up against my feet.

Appearances to the contrary, our soldiers with the poles were directing our craft and turning the will of the tide to our profit, and at last we were on the shore. Safe in our wet ambulance, we started on our way again. I was never so cold, so wet, so everything wretched in my life, and what should Lieutenant Johnston do but propose to go out of our way to see St. Peter's Church.

"An old colonial relic," he said. "You ladies ought not to miss it now that you are so near."

"I don't want to see any relics," I answered promptly. "The only thing I want to see is a fire and something to eat."

But he would drive out of our way to show us that old church. I was too wretched and miserable to look at it with proper interest. I don't remember how it looked - I only know that I had to go there and see it whether I would or no. George Washington had done something or other there - got married, I believe. I think the church had some very fine ivy on it, but I am not sure. I thought it was old and small, and that it might do very well in summer, but that under present circumstances Washington himself would forgive me for being wholly in the thought of getting to a fire. Hunger and cold, cramped positions and rain dripping in on me had blunted everything in me except longings for creature comforts. The lieutenant drove all around the church religiously before starting on our way again.

"I don't believe you saw it at all," he said to me with real concern.

"Oh, yes, I did!" I answered promptly, terrified lest we should be turned back to look at it again, "I saw it thoroughly."

Of course, Milicent had looked the old church over and talked intelligently about it, but for the life of me, I couldn't remember whether it was made of brick or wood. And I didn't care, either.

The rain had dwindled into a drizzle, night was coming on, and I began to grow more and more anxious to find a stopping-place.

"I do hope we shall get into a place where they keep good fires," I said. "If we should get into a place where they burn green pine, I should lie down and die. Wet, green pine," I continued dolorously, "that smokes and never burns, and raw, clammy biscuit is about what we'll get tonight."

The lieutenant looked as if he was very sorry for me.

"I wish," he said unhappily, "I wish I knew how to tell a place where they burn green pine." Suddenly he brightened.

"I have it!" he exclaimed. "We won't stop at any house where there isn't a big wood-pile. We don't stop anywhere until we find a big white house, a big wood-pile and a nigger chopping wood."

We passed several dwellings, but the lieutenant wouldn't stop. "I don't see any wood-pile," or "The wood-pile ain't big enough," he would say.

At last we came upon what we wanted - a large white

house, a wood-pile nearly as high as the house and a negro man chopping wood for dear life.

Through a big front yard full of shrubbery, a wide graveled walk and circular drive-way led up to the house, and in a few minutes our ambulance was in front of the veranda. The lieutenant sprang out and went up the steps.

A gray-headed negro butler answered his knock.

"Wanter see master, sah? Yes, sah. Won't you step right in, sah?"

"I haven't time to stop a minute unless I can get lodgings for the night. I have ladies in the ambulance. Ask your master if he will be good enough to see me at the door for a minute."

Sambo bowed, made haste backward, and almost immediately an old gentleman appeared.

"Certainly, sir, certainly," he said, interrupting the lieutenant in the middle of his application. "Bring the ladies right in, sir."

And he helped to bring us in himself. Servants of all kinds appeared as if by magic from all quarters, and took charge of our trunks, satchels, ambulance, and driver.

The Virginia gentleman of those days was hospitable, as men are truthful, for his own sake first. His hospitality was spontaneous, unconscious, and free as heaven itself with its favors. All it asked in return was that you should come when you pleased, go when you pleased, stay as long as you pleased, and enjoy yourself to the top of your bent.

The house was a house of spindle-legged chairs, spindle-legged piano, brass fire-dogs, fine dark woodwork, candelabra of brass and crystal, and tall wax candles. Through the gloom the eyes of old portraits looked down upon us. In the wide fireplace of our bedroom crackled a mighty fire of oak and hickory; over the fire hung a bright brass kettle singing merrily; there were the ever-present fire-dogs and fender of burnished brass, and on the mantle two wax lights burning in silver candlesticks. Two smiling negro maids stood ready to minister to us.

In opposite corners of the room stood two large, canopied, mahogany bedsteads, with great, downy feather-beds and counterpanes, sheets and pillows as white as snow and smelling of lavender. The undiminished length of the table at which we sat down that night bore testimony not only to the good cheer it had given, but to that which it was ready to give. It was of dark rich mahogany, polished to the fineness of a mirror, that reflected the tall silver candlesticks holding wax candles. The silver service and beautiful old china rested on white mats that were not visible except where encircling fringes of gleaming damask suggested nests of snores. On a quaint buffet stood cut-glass decanters holding topaz and ruby wines and brandy arid whisky.

The great mahogany sideboard - a small house in itself - nearly reached the ceiling The upper half was a cabinet with glass doors shaped like the doors of a Gothic cathedral. The lower half had drawers with white knobs, and bellied doors of the most beautiful dark wood, reflecting, like the table, the glow of the wax lights. The glass cabinet glittered with silver and crystal, and here and there was clouded with the rich maroon and saffron of rare old china. Our hostess was a stately and beautiful old lady in black silk (much torn), with fichu and cuffs of real old lace. Our host wore fine black broadcloth, threadbare and of ancient cut.

Such a soft, shining picture as that supper- room was! I wish I could paint it as I saw it that night! And what a delicious supper! There was tea, sure enough; tea of delicious aroma; and sure enough sugar, too, in fine white lumps which had to be picked up with silver tongs. There were little tea-cakes and fairy-like puffs and wafers, and delicious hot rolls! creamy and velvety, and light as a breath.

In crystal dishes gleamed the rich, clear red and amber of preserved fruits, and crystal-clear sweetmeats were set before us in crystal dishes. These were cut in designs of leaf and flower, fish and bird, squirrels, rabbits, and acorns - really too elaborately cut and too beautifully transparent to be eaten.

And then there was Virginia fried chicken - of such a delicate rich brown! and such juicy sweetness! At last we each lay covered up in a great downy bed, and went to sleep, and slept as if we never expected to wake up.

Chapter XI

THE OLD ORDER

WE found fresh straw and hot bricks in the bottom of our ambulance when we were ready to leave the next morning, an excellent luncheon and two bottles of wine. Soon after we started the wind changed, the clouds disappeared, and the sun came out. By the time we reached the Chickahominy there was sunshine in plenty - and wind, too.

Not a boat was in sight, and no figure on either bank of man or beast. I thought the lieutenant and the driver would split their lungs hallooing, but there was no response. Nobody answered and nobody came. We waited on the bank an hour without seeing anybody. Then an Indian came by in a skiff and we hailed him. He paddled to the shore, and we asked him if he knew where we could get a boat and some one to put us across.

He knew of nothing and nobody of the kind within reach.

"I must hire your skiff then," said the lieutenant.

The Indian grinned.

"You no get cross in it. You spill out."

"Never mind that, so you get paid for your skiff. I am an old sailor."

Powhatan didn't think the lieutenant could manage that skiff; however, he got his price and gave in.

When he saw the three of us squeezing ourselves into the skiff he remonstrated again.

"Squaws spill out. Squaws git sick," he insisted. He told the lieutenant that we would be frightened out of our lives before we got across the river. He didn't know that Millie and I had been brought up on the coast and were as used to water as ducks.

Whoever has rowed an Indian skiff may have some idea of what a cockle-shell it was that took us across the Chickahominy. I sat in one end, Milicent in the other, and Lieutenant Johnston in the middle, paddle in hand, while our little craft switched and wriggled and rocked itself about in a manner that was as extraordinary as it was dangerous, and that was nearer perpetual motion than anything I ever saw.

At last the lieutenant stood up and straddled the boat to balance her. How he ever balanced himself I can't say, but he stood with one foot on each of her sides and managed her somehow. No one but an old sailor could have done it. I expected every minute to see him fall over into the water.

The sun was shining down, silvering the waters of the Chickahominy. The strong winds churned the waves and blew our hats and veils almost off our heads, and almost blew our breath away - when the rocking skiff left us any. And out on the wide, turbulent, bright river we tossed and tumbled, and laughed and got wet and came near drowning. I never had more fun in any sail. But at last we were safely across, and waiting by the York River Railroad for our train. The half-breed gave us our trunks, and took back his skiff and our money. In a few hours we were in Richmond, where the lieutenant saw us to our hotel, and left. I sent a letter by him to Dan, begging Dan's pardon for having my own way.

The next day found us in Petersburg. Our business here was to provide ourselves with money with which to buy Yankee goods - particularly a Confederate uniform - in Yankeeland. I wanted as much gold as our broker could let me have, but he advised me against taking more than enough to make the trip with, and a small margin for contingencies.

"It will be in your way and increase your danger," he said. "Confederate notes will get you to the Potomac. From there you need a little gold to take you to Baltimore. After you are there I will contrive any sum you want to your trustees in Norfolk. They, being inside the Yankee lines, can send it to Baltimore."

Our next objective point was Mrs. Rixey's in Culpeper. Blockade-runners were continually setting out from there, and we thought we would have no difficulty in attaching ourselves to a party. After a rest in Petersburg of a day and a half, we started for Culpeper, reaching Mrs. Rixey's at nightfall. We told her husband that we wanted to join a party of blockade-runners.

"Mrs. Otis and her two daughters start north to-morrow; perhaps you can go with them," he said, and went out to see about it.

Unfortunately - or fortunately - the Otis party was complete - there was no vacant seat in their wagon.

"I will be on the lookout for you," Mr. Rixey said. "Somebody else will be along soon."

Before breakfast he knocked at our door.

"There are two gentlemen downstairs who are going north," he said, when Millie stuck her head out. "They give their names as Captain Locke and Mr. Holliway, and they seem to be gentlemen. That is all I know about them. You might see them and talk the matter over."

We finished dressing hurriedly and went down to the parlor, where we met Captain Locke and Mr. Holliway, and after a brief talk decided to go with them.

The best vehicle we could get was a wagon without springs, and instead of a body four planks laid across the axles, one plank set up on each side, and no ends at all.

Over the rude floor we had a quantity of straw piled, and two chairs were set up for Milicent and me. The gentlemen seated themselves on our baggage, which consisted of two small trunks into which we had crowded a few articles for each of them. The wagoner, a rough mountaineer, sat on a plank which had been laid across the two uprights at the sides.

It was a bitterly cold day. Milicent and I wore thick

cloaks, and the wagoner supplied a blanket which we wrapped about our feet. In addition, the gentlemen contributed a large blanket shawl which they insisted upon folding about our shoulders, declaring that their overcoats protected them sufficiently. Now and then they got out of the wagon and walked and stamped to keep their legs from getting stiff with cold, and at last Milicent and I were reduced to the same device for keeping up our circulation. We got so stiff we couldn't move, and the gentlemen had to lift us out of the wagon, pull us about and drag us into a walk and a run.

It was dark when we reached the house at which it had been suggested we should stop. Lights were in every window and we could see much moving about. Mr. Holliway went in to ask for lodgings.

He returned quickly and jumped into the wagon, saying to the wagoner:

"Drive on."

Milicent and I were almost freezing.

"What's the matter?" we asked in keen disappointment.

Just then the wagon made a turn, and we saw distinctly into the house through an uncurtained window. There was a long white object in the middle of the floor and over it stood a weeping woman.

"Why," I exclaimed, "somebody's dead there."

"Yes, I didn't want to tell you," he said. "It's a dead soldier. I was afraid it might make you feel badly. Ladies are sometimes superstitious, and I feared you might take it as a bad omen for our journey."

But we found out afterward that it was he who had taken it for a bad omen. He was going north to see his family, and he was so anxious about them that he talked of little else. Captain Locke's mission was not so clear. He called it business - we little knew what dangerous business it was! - and we troubled our heads no further about it.

It was very late when we at last came upon a tumbledown farmhouse, where we were taken in for the night. The family who lived there did their best for us, but they were far from being comfortable themselves. By this time, however, any quarters and any fare were acceptable. We slept in the room with a goodly company, all fortunately of our own sex, and the gentlemen, as we heard afterward, in even more crowded quarters.

Our poverty-stricken hosts did not wish to charge us, but before we left the next morning we insisted upon paying them.

That morning a little Jew boy was added to our party. Just how, or when, or where we picked him up, I can not recall, and I should probably never have thought of him again if he had not impressed himself upon me most unpleasantly afterward at Berlin.

Our second night we spent according to our program, in Fauquier County, with Mr. Robert Bolling, a friend of my husband's.

"I am astonished at your trying to run the blockade, Mrs. Grey," he said.

"Why?" I asked. "And why are you more astonished at me than at Milicent?"

I had been hearing similar remarks, and was becoming curious.

"Because you look like a little girl. I am surprised at such nerve in so youthful a lady."

"I want a new uniform for Dan," I said "He's promoted."

Mr. Bolling laughed heartily.

"And I am quite as brave as Milicent," I insisted.

"Well, I am surprised at you both. It is a dangerous undertaking."

Our wagoner was invited to take supper with us. He was rough and ill-clad, and he felt out of place, but Mr. Bolling charmed him into ease and talked over our prospective journey with him.

"It is well for you to be on good terms with your wagoner," he said to us privately when he sent out the invitation.

Mr. Bolling was old and gray-haired, or would have been in the field. His home was one of the most celebrated country-seats in Fauquier, and he himself full of honors and one of the best-known men in the State.

The night we spent at this old Virginia homestead was repetition of a night previously described, with variations. Here were the same old-fashioned mahogany furniture with claw feet and spindle legs, and wax lights in brass and silver candelabra, and rare old china, and some heirlooms whose history we were interested in. Several of these had come with the first Bollings from England. There was a sword which had come down from the War of the Roses, and on the wall, in a place of special honor, hung the sword of a Bolling who had distinguished himself in the Revolution. Mr. Bolling took it down and laid it in Milicent's outstretched hands with a smile.

"I am a believer in State's rights, and I am a Secessionist, I suppose," said the old man with a sigh, as he hung the sword back in its place. "But - I hate to fight the old flag. I hate that."

Above the sword was the portrait of the Bolling who had worn the sword, a soldierly looking fellow in the uniform of a Revolutionary colonel.

"He saved the old flag once at the cost of his life," the aged man said, sighing again. "He is buried out yonder in the graveyard, wrapped in the folds of the very flag he snatched from the hands of the British. If we were to open his grave to-night, we would find his bones and ashes wrapped in that flag he died to save. Yes, I am sorry to fight the old flag."

"Then," I said innocently and without thinking, "it is well that you are exempted from service in the field."

His eyes flashed.

"Ah, no, my dear! Since fighting there is, I wish I could be in it. If I were young enough and strong enough I'd take that sword down and follow Robert Lee. Virginia is invaded."

Chapter XII

A Dangerous Masquerade

THE night of our third day found us at the wagoner's cottage on the top of the Blue Ridge Mountains. As we climbed our slow and painful way up to the ruddy little light that beckoned us from its wild and eerie perch, moonlight and starlight fell upon snow-capped cliffs and into deep valleys, touching them into solemn, mystical beauty. It was as if we had lost ourselves in the clear, white stillness of the enchanted Snow Kingdom that had enthralled and terrified us in the happy days of fairy tales. But there was nothing magical about the cottage when we finally got there, or the welcome, or the supper. Instead of fairies and cowslip dew and bread of lily pollen, we had a delightfully wholesome, plump Virginia housewife, a Virginia welcome, and, above all, a Virginia supper.

The cottage was plainly furnished, but it was neat as a pin. The mountaineer's wife and mother served us, the one waiting on us, the other cooking. We sat at table in the kitchen, and such a feast as we had! There was nice apple-butter on the table, and delicious milk and cream, fresh eggs and hot buckwheat cakes, and genuine maple sirup, of course. I have never tasted such buckwheats anywhere. And how fast the old lady fried them, and the wife handed them to us, piping hot! and how fast we ate! and how many!

The furniture in our bedroom, as everywhere else, was exceedingly plain, but so deliciously clean. And such a bed! such a downy, fragrant bed! The sheets were snowy, the coverlet was spotless. As I went to sleep I had an idea that the feathers in that bed must have come from the breasts of mountain birds that had never touched the earth. In the morning the mountaineer took us to a point near his house, where we could stand and look into - I have forgotten how many States, and out upon snowy peaks, and mountain streams, and lovely shadowed vales.

We lost our Confederate captain when we started down the mountain that day; Mr. Holliway had all along been in civilian's dress, and now Captain Locke changed his uniform for citizen's clothes, leaving the uniform at the cottage, to be called for on his return.

The fourth night we reached Berryville.

Here it was necessary to hold a council with closed doors, for the presence of the little Jew boy had for several days prevented us from talking freely.

He seemed to have eyes and ears all over him, and we felt vaguely that he would use both to our disadvantage. So we shut him out of the little room at the inn in Berryville where we held our secret council. The morrow would find us inside the Federal lines - it was necessary to prepare our story. We agreed that Captain Locke was to be our brother, because he had fair hair and blue eyes like ourselves. Mr. Holliway was of too entirely different a type to be claimed for a nearer relationship than that of cousin. We were young ladies of Baltimore who had been visiting at Mr. Robert Bolling's in Fauquier, and our brother and cousin had come south to take us home, not being willing that we should undertake such a journey alone. Captain Locke gave Milicent some papers to be concealed in the lining of her muff. I, too, had some papers to hide for him. Fortunately we did not know until afterward that Captain Locke was a Confederate spy, and that the papers we carried were official documents of importance to the Confederacy, and that if discovered the captain would be strung up in short order and every one of us sent to prison.

If we had known what he was and the nature of the

papers, I think our patriotism would have risen to the occasion, but we should have been more nervous and more likely to betray ourselves. So I think he was wise to take the liberty of counting on our patriotism, and also to keep us in the dark as a safeguard for both ourselves and the papers.

The next forenoon we reached the Potomac River, and found ourselves in Federal lines. Our wagoner bade us good-by and left us there on the bank. In the river below lay the lighter on which we were to cross the Potomac. It was crowded with Federal soldiers. There was no way to reach it except to slide down the bank, and the bank was steep. To slide down, it was neither a graceful nor a dignified thing to do. I drew back.. The captain took me by the hand to pull me over. I still drew back. I did not want to slide down that bank.

"Come on, sister!" he exclaimed with brotherly crossness.

I grinned broadly, but the captain, his back to the lighter, gave me such a serious look that I sobered in an instant.

"Sister, come along! Don't be a goose!" he said, and giving me a jerk pulled me over.

The Federal soldiers on the lighter could see and hear. One blunder now and we were lost. I yielded to the inevitable and slid down the bank with the captain; Mr. Holliway followed with Milicent. Another minute, and we stood on the lighter in the midst of Yankee soldiers and Yankee horses. A horse's nose was over my shoulder the whole way. Soldiers were crowded up against me there was ample occasion for swears, but I don't think I heard an oath the entire distance, and they were courtesy itself to Milicent and me.

Landing at Berlin, we walked into the office of the provost marshal. The provost was out, and the deputy who was at his desk looked at us with cool, inquisitive eyes. He put the usual questions and received ready-made answers.

"Who are you?" he asked Captain Locke in a very suspicious tone.

"Charles D. Moore, of Baltimore."

"Occupation?"

"I am studying law."

"Humph!" with a glance that made me keenly alive to the lameness of that story told by the martial-looking captain.

"What are you doing down here?"

"Taking my sisters back home."

"Humph! Who are you?" turning to Mr. Holliway.

"William H. May, of Baltimore."

"Studying law too?"

"No. I expect to study medicine."

"Are you taking these ladies back home too?"

"I am accompanying them, certainly," said Mr. Holliway with asperity.

"Who are these ladies?"

"My sisters," said Captain Locke firmly, "and I am here to protect them on their way back home."

"Where have they been?"

"They are from Mr. Robert Bolling's in Fauquier County, Virginia. They have been visiting at his house. We wished them to return to Baltimore, and I came south for them. My cousin, Mr. May, joined us."

"And you - what are you doing down here?" with a touch of irony to Holliway

"Got caught this side by the war, and and trying to get back home."

"Ah, yes, of course. I can't pass you. Take seats, please. The marshal will be in directly."

Our evidence was too smooth.

It was plain the deputy didn't believe in us, and we felt uneasy and miserable to the soles of our boots - except Captain Locke, who looked thoroughly at his ease.

It was an hour or longer before the marshal came in. It seemed a great deal more, yet I can't say that I longed to see him.

"What's all this?" he asked his deputy as he took in our party, braced up against the wall.

"A party who crossed from Virginia this morning. They

have been visiting in Fauquier - they say - and want to get back to Baltimore. A lame tale, I call it. I would send them straight back if I had my way with them."

The provost's eyes had rested first on me, as I happened to be more conspicuously placed than the others. I have been accredited with a most ingenuous countenance. I returned his gaze with a regard utterly "childlike and bland," looking up into his face with eyes as frank and trusting as a baby's. Past me his gaze went to Milicent - I have said before that Milicent had the face of a Madonna; then the manly and straightforward eyes of Locke held him; and last Mr. Holliway's reserved and gentlemanly countenance met his scrutiny with a quiet dignity that disarmed suspicion. He began by interviewing Milicent and me. When he questioned me I said plaintively:

"I have been here an hour, sir, and I am, very tired. I would be so much obliged if you would send us on home I am almost sick with the journey I have taken, and I should so like to get home to-night."

"That is impossible," he said; "but," he continued kindly, "I do not think you will be detained later than to-morrow morning."

He conversed in a low tone with his deputy, and then I heard him say: "Let them spend the night at the old German's on the hill, and tomorrow we will see about it."

Then turning to us, he said that an orderly would conduct us to a place where we would be lodged for the night. When an officer asked about our baggage, I extended my keys quickly, saying:

"We have two small trunks."

He took the keys with an apology. As I was passing out of the door I turned back and held out my satchel.

"I forgot that you have to examine this."

"It is not necessary, miss," he said, smiling.

The old Dutchman was out, but his wife received us and made us comfortable. While we were at supper he came in. "I speeks mit you after supper," he said solemnly, and sat in silence until we had finished.

Then he took us into a room, closed and locked the door, came close to us, and whispered:

"I knows dat you haf run te plockate. You bees in ver' mooch tancher. Town te stdreet I hears you vas at mine house, unt I hears ver' mooch talk, unt I lis'en. I vill help you if you vill let me."

He now addressed himself particularly to Captain Locke and Mr. Holliway:

"You, shentlemen, mus' leave mine house, shoost as soon as you can, or you vill be daken prisoners. I vill help you to get avay."

"We can't do it," said Locke promptly. "I can not leave my sisters alone and unprotected."

Milicent and I were trembling with fear.

"Brother," said Milicent, "you and Cousin William must leave us and save yourselves."

"Please go," I begged. I could not keep my eyes off the door. I feared every moment to hear the rap of the sergeant come to arrest our friends. But the captain and Mr. Holliway reiterated their determination not to leave us in our present situation. If I had not been scared almost to death I could have laughed at the perfect brotherliness of Locke's protestations.

"Tere is tancher, shentlemen. I hears te talk town te street," urged the Dutchman with every appearance of earnestness and good-will.

"What did you hear?" asked Locke nonchalantly.

"Oh, tey finks you hat not tolt vat you vast Tey finks you be Secesh - unt I ton's know vat fey finks."

"I can't help what they think," said Locke. "I am going to protect my sisters."

"How you brotect tem ven you be brisoners, hein?"

"I don't know," answered Locke, smiling, "but I certainly shall not leave them."

"Vat goot you do? I vill take care of te ladies. Nopody vill hu't tem, unt I vill see dat tey gets off all right. Tere is no tancher for tem."

"Thank you, my friend," said the captain simply and heartily. "But we can not accept your kind offer. We must take my sisters home ourselves."

"I ver' sorry," said the Dutchman sadly.

As soon as the door closed behind him, we began to plead.

"Captain," said Milicent, "you and Mr. Holliway must go. We will not consent to anything else."

"We should be regular deserters to do that," said Locke contemptuously. "I think the old fellow is exaggerating. Or maybe he is pumping us. Holliway and I will walk down the street and see."

We thought this was madness, and we were miserable from the moment they left until they were safely back. Captain Locke was, as always, at his ease, but Mr. Holliway was very pale. He knew, as Milicent and I did not, the risk we were all running, and he was more concerned perhaps for Locke's safety than for his own. For him arrest meant prison at the worst - for Locke, a halter.

"The Dutchman is right," he said in answer to our questions. "We stopped outside several places and heard them talking about us and our arrest. We are practically prisoners."

He tried to speak cheerfully and as if it would be a sure and easy matter to find some way out of our predicament; but the truth was that he had been struggling all along against great depression of spirits; his health was bad, the incident of the first night of our journey had impressed him, and he had evidently felt himself under a cloud ever since our experience at the provost's.

"That talk doesn't amount to much," said Captain Locke carelessly.

The room in which we were sitting was that which had been taken for Milicent's and my bedroom. Captain Locke got up, walked to the door and locked it.

"You have needles and thread, I think, ladies?" Milicent and I immediately produced them.

and slipped on our thimbles. He handed Milicent his open knife.

"Rip the papers out of your muff, Mrs. Norman, and you, little madam, let me have those I gave you."

The two I had were hidden in my sleeve. While Milicent and I were getting the papers out, I heard Mr. Holliway say:

"Burn those papers, Locke. You can never get them to Baltimore, and you know in what fearful peril they keep us."

"I might as well turn back if I burn them," said the captain. "I take those papers to Baltimore, or I die trying - and I won't die."

"Excuse the trouble I give you, ladies," he said, leaning back in his chair and putting his feet on another. "Will you open the hems of my trousers and sew those papers inside? It is a great favor."

We ripped each hem, folded the papers inside as flat as possible, and sewed the hems up again. I had not made over Dan's old uniform for nothing, and Milicent was always a skilful needlewoman - our hems looked quite natural and not at all "stuffed." But we were so nervous that we worked very slowly, for we felt that a wrong stitch might cost Captain Locke his life.

He had worn his trousers turned up around the bottom to keep them out of the mud. When we had finished he carefully turned them back again, Mr. Holliway looking on gloomily.

"Now, ladies," said the captain cheerfully, "we will all retire and get a good night's rest. You have had a hard day and I am sure you must be tired."

"Aren't you going away?" we asked anxiously. "What did you take the papers for?"

He smiled.

"Little madam," he said, "you had best go to bed and get a good night's rest. That is what I am going to do. Mrs. Norman, make this poor child go to bed. And you will promise me to try to rest too, won't you?"

There was a rap on the door.

Chapter XIII

A Last Farewell

MR. HOLLIWAY opened it to admit the Dutchman.

"Shentlemen," he began earnestly, "tey haf got te leetle Chew poy trunk mit giffin' him visky, unt he hat tolt every-ding. I pe your vrent. You mus' get avay pefore mitnight."

"The little Jew knows nothing to tell," said the captain. "His drunken babble is not worth attention. We can not leave my sisters."

"How you help tem by stayin'? I gif you my vort dat tey vill get to Paltimore all right. I hates to see tem Yankees takes you up in mine house."

Milicent and I believed in the German. So I think did both gentlemen by this time, but we had come this far under their care, and they were loath to leave us unless entirely convinced that it was for our safety as well as their own. Mr. Holliway was no less concerned about us than Captain Locke was, but he took a darker view of the situation. He drew Locke aside and they talked together in low tones. I caught the word "reckless" and "those papers," and "a disadvantage to them," "safer without us." When they turned back to us Captain Locke said:

"We leave the question in your hands, ladies. Perhaps we - and more particularly I - endanger you by remaining. But I hate to leave you alone this way, and I am not afraid of anything that can happen to me. If the worst came to the worst, and we were arrested, I have some influence in the North which might still be of benefit to us all."

"Use it for yourself and Mr. Holliway," we said, "and go."

"Think well, ladies. You want us to go now, but when we are gone and you are here alone, won't you feel desolate and deserted?"

"We will only be glad you're gone", I said.

"I don't think I ever heard such a polite speech in my life," said Captain Locke, laughing. "Holliway, I think we had better leave immediately."

He stood cool and smiling, but Mr. Holliway, whose health was not robust, and upon whom the hardships of the journey and the excitement had told, was ghastly. Not that he lacked courage. He would have stayed and died for us, as far as that was concerned; but his physical endurance was not great, and from the first he had been oppressed with a presentiment of evil.

Milicent had drawn Captain Locke aside, and was urging him to go, as I knew, and, as I think, to destroy the papers which Holliway felt imperiled him. He gave her a smiling negative.

"You must go yourself, and please help us make the captain go," I was saying to Mr. Holliway.

"You will have to do that," he replied. "I have said what I could. It is madness for us to stay, as I am thoroughly convinced now. You would be safer without us. Locke doesn't think so, but I know it. His character and the papers he carries increase the danger for us all."

Captain Locke and Milicent had finished their conference.

"We will go," he said quietly. "A pen and ink, my friend," to the Dutchman.

"Make haste and go," we pleaded.

But he waited for the pen and ink.

"We have time enough," he said, consulting his watch very coolly. "It is not yet half-past eleven."

He wrote a note and gave it to the Dutchman to be mailed that night.

"If you get into any trouble," he said to Milicent, "telegraph to this address."

And he gave her a slip of paper on which was written: "Gov. - , Baltimore, Md."

"The letter is to my uncle, and if you are in any trouble he will help you out. The Governor will be advised of your situation, and a telegram to him will be understood."

"Good night, ladies, and au revoir," he said gaily, bowing over our hands. "We will meet in Baltimore."

"I echo that," said Mr. Holliway with assumed cheerfulness. "It has been a great pleasure and privilege to know you, ladies. With all its shadows, this journey will always be one of my sweetest memories."

We might never see them again. We knew it as we looked into Locke's bonnie blue eyes and Holliway's dark sad ones. They had been our brave and gentle knights, shielding us and enduring all the hardships cheerfully. One of them was weaker, we knew, because he had given his blanket to keep us warm. We looked bravely back into the two brave faces that looked into ours - one sign of faltering and they would not leave us.

"I will say a 'Hail Mary' for each of you every night," I said.

"I, too," said Milicent softly.

"Thank you," there was a quiver in each voice now. "We will try to deserve your prayers, dear ladies."

Then they bowed themselves out with smiling faces. One of them we never saw again.

Chapter XIV

THE LITTLE JEW BOY AND THE PROVOST'S DEPUTY

THE Dutchman went with them to show them the way he said they must take. His wife came in and gossiped with us.

According to her account, it was a miracle that we had passed through the provost's hands as well as we had.

"If de vimmins had peen dere, dey vould hat pult your close off, unt dey vould haf search you all ofer. I ton't know as you haf anyding you not vent dem to see, but if you hat anyding, tey pe zhure to fint it. Te vimmins tat hat to pe dere to- tay vas gone avay somevare. If she had peen dere, you vas hat harter times tan you vas hat."

I thought with a shudder of our muffs and satchels, our pictures in Confederate uniform, and those papers.

"Mine man say some yolks vas arrested town te river to-tay. Dere vas dree laties unt van shentleman. Tey dry to cross at de Point of Vrocks [Point of Rocks] unt fey vas took up unt sent pack."

"What were their names?" we asked eagerly.

We remembered that the Otis party consisted of three ladies and one gentleman. We had kept in sight of their ambulance for some time. But at the parting of our ways, when they had taken one road and we another, our driver had said: "They are going to try to get across at the Point of Rocks, and they'll sure be turned back or took up, one."

"I ton't know vat dere names," said the Dutchwoman. "Mine man vill know. He forgets notding."

When he came in he thought a little, and then he said he thought the name was "Odis." So we had been luckier than we thought in the chance that prevented us from joining their party.

The old German had directed our friends as best he could, and started them on their way. They were to keep to the woods and walk to Frederick, from where, he thought, they might reach Baltimore. He told us that they had not gone away immediately after leaving us, although he had urged them to do so. They had said they wouldn't go away until they saw how we took being left alone. They had gone around to the window of the room in which we were sitting, and had spied upon us. When they saw us gossiping with the old woman, they had gone off satisfied that we would not break down after their departure.

"Tey vas not so vraid vor her," he said, indicating Milicent. "It vas you, te leetle matam, as he call you, dat he vas vraid vor. He vraid you vould cry pecause you vas so leetle, unt pecause you vas so ver' younk. I ask him vat he do if you cry, unt I dry to make him come avay, unt he say: 'If she cry I von't go. I vill go in tat room unt I vill cake her up in mine arms unt I vill not stop until I put her safe in Captain Grey's arms! Dot is vot I vill do.' He titn't leaf you off," to Milicent, "put he dort you pe mo' prave."

If he had been at the window then he would have seen tears in our eyes. But I bore a grudge.

"Milicent," I said, as soon as we were alone, "I don't see why people should make of me just the exception that they always do. I may be a little younger, but I am married, and I have got just as much sense about some things and I'm just as brave as you are. I'm a soldier's wife, the wife of a Confederate officer. I wonder how I have behaved that everybody expects me to be a coward."

And Milicent comforted me.

The next morning an orderly rapped at the door of the German's house and asked for us.

The German answered.

"Tell the ladies," with an emphasis on the word, "the provost says they can go on, The train leaves in fifteen minutes. They will find their bagagge at the station. Here are their keys."

"You see it is vell tat te shentlemen tit not vait vor bermission," said the German as we hurried into our wraps.

We heard afterward that following our departure a sergeant-at-arms called for the "shentlemen." Our train was late coming in. As we stood on the platform waiting we saw that wretched little Jew boy fooling around and watching us. We pretended not to see him. Suddenly I felt a tremor in Milicent's arm which was linked in mine.

"Do you see who is on the platform talking with the little Jew boy? No, don't turn your head - don't look suddenly - don't look at all. It is the provost's deputy who didn't believe in us yesterday."

Oh, if the train would only come, and we were on it and gone! As it rolled up beside the platform we had to restrain ourselves from getting on it too eagerly. But we were at last in our seats; the whistle blew, and the train moved out of the station.

The station was behind us, out of sight, and we were leaning back enjoying ourselves, when Milicent glanced behind her. I was looking out of the window when I felt her hand on my arm.

"Don't look suddenly. But when you can, glance behind us."

Three seats behind us sat the provosts deputy. He was reading a paper, or, rather, watching us over a paper which he held up before him. He kept us under close observation the whole way. We had no opportunity to consult about the difficulties of the situation, but we felt that we were to elude our shadow in Baltimore or not at all. Carriages stood thick around the depot. Drivers were cracking their whips and importuning the public for patronage. We stepped off the platform into the midst of them, got to haggling about prices, and found ourselves mixed up in a lot of carriages, the yelling and screaming drivers having closed up behind us around the platform to which they had turned their attention. There we saw the deputy's hat revolving rapidly, as if he were turning himself about to catch sight of us. Chance stood our friend. We happened to stand between two carriages, the doors of which hung open. A party of two ladies stepped into one. Instantly we took the other.

"Drive fast to No. - Charles Street," Milicent said to the driver. Several carriages rolled out of the depot with our own, and before we reached Mrs. Harris's we felt that we had escaped the deputy. Once with mother and Bobby we forgot him.

Chapter XV

I Fall Into The Hands Of The Enemy

MRS. HARRIS kept a select and fashionable boarding-house. There were many regular boarders and a stream of people coming and going all the time. She was a Southern sympathizer, and her house was a hotbed of sedition and intrigue for both sides. Among her guests were three Yankee officers, whom I made up my mind - or, rather, my mind needed no making up - to dislike. Uniform and all, I objected to them. The day after we came Mrs. Harris was chatting with us in mother's room.

"I must introduce you to those Federal officers who are in the house," she remarked.

"I beg you will not!" I replied indignantly. "I will have nothing to do with them."

"Then you will make a grave mistake, my child. That course would betray you at once. You've put your head into the lion's mouth, and prudence is the better policy until you get it out again. If you meet these officers and are civil to them they may be of assistance to you when you want to go back."

Accordingly, when our household met as usual in the parlors that evening, Captain Hosmer, Assistant Adjutant-General William D. Whipple, of Schenck's command, and Major Brooks - also, I think, of Schenck's command - were presented to me.

Major Brooks had such a keen, satirical way of looking at

me that I immediately took a violent prejudice against him, though I tried hard to conceal it. Schenck's adjutant I did not like much better. Captain Hosmer was objectionable on general principles as a Yankee, but he was really a handsome fellow and a most charming gentleman, and though I had hard work overcoming my prejudices sufficiently to be quite civil at first, I ended by becoming warmly attached to him. My impulse was to avoid these gentlemen and to show my colors in a passive way. I say in a passive way, because anything approaching discourtesy Dan would have condemned. On duty, he would have shot a Yankee down quickly enough; off duty, he would never have failed in politeness to a gentleman in any uniform. As I could not well appear here as a Confederate officer's wife, I was introduced to these gentlemen as Miss Duncan The day after our arrival we mailed Captain Locke's picture, which he had given us for the purpose, to his sister in Harrisburg, and called to see Mr. Holliway's mother and sisters. They were charming women, and entertained us in true Baltimore fashion.

Indeed, I soon found myself in a whirl of gaiety. Mrs. Harris's house was a merry one. Of course, being in Baltimore, its politics were mixed, as we have said, but as far as social position and culture were concerned, the guests were above reproach. The parlors in the evening reminded one of those of a fashionable pleasure resort.

Next door was another boarding-house. Mother's windows overlooked the entrance, and we amused ourselves - according to boarding - house custom and privilege by watching our own and our neighbors' callers and guests, and by nicknaming them. There was one of the next-door boarders who entertained us greatly. We dubbed him "the Professor." He had a funny way of wearing his green goggles as if they were about to fall off his nose. He had long, snaky curls which looked very greasy and glossy, and he walked with a slight stoop, using a goldheaded cane; and he always carried a book under his arm.

In our own house were two ladies who afforded us much amusement. They were sisters, as Captain Hosmer took occasion to inform me early in our acquaintance, but they were politically so opposed to each other that they did not speak.

Mrs. Bonds was a black Republican, Mrs. Lineman a red-hot rebel. This latter fact we discovered by degrees. Women did not gossip in those days - not to talk was a necessary evil - very evil and very necessary in a boarding- house of mixed politics in Baltimore during war times.

Mrs. Harris kept a private parlor for herself and daughters, and here we poor rebels met every now and then with a little less restraint, though even here we had to be very careful. One day a note was brought me.

"Happy greetings, dear friends! Can you arrange without inconvenience to yourselves for me to call, and will you allow me that pleasure? Do not hesitate to decline if you feel so disposed. I will understand.

"L."

There was no other signature, but we knew the hand. Thank God! He was alive and well! We took the note to Mrs. Harris. Of course we would see him if we could make a way. After a little consultation it was arranged that we receive him in the little parlor upstairs. We addressed an envelope to ourselves, put a blank sheet of paper in it, sealed it, and enclosed it in a note to the captain. The latter we did not know how to address; we were merely to give it to his messenger, who was waiting. We wrote:

"Delighted. Come to side entrance at half- past eight; present enclosed and you will be shown up.

"N. & M."

At half-past eight we were waiting in Mrs. Harris's private parlor - there were several ladies there beside ourselves. Of all nights, why couldn't they keep away this night? - when Mrs. Harris's maid brought up the envelope we had addressed to ourselves.

"Show him up," we said.

Why in the world wouldn't those other women go? And would there be any callers in the private parlor to-night?

"Dr. Moreau!" announced Mrs. Harris's maid.

Into the room walked the "Professor," green goggles and all. Who in the world was he coming to see? What was he doing here any way? And on this night of all nights when we were looking for Captain Locke and wishing for as few witnesses as possible! Through the open door behind the "Professor," we caught a glimpse of Mrs. Bonds out in the hall, following him with curious eyes. If we could only slip downstairs and keep the captain from coming up to-night! And why didn't the girl bring the captain in? Milicent was rising to go out into the hall, when the "Professor," having glanced around the room, approached us.

"I was invited to call on some ladies here this evening? Am I in the wrong room?" said a perfectly strange voice, the voice you would expect to hear from a fossil.

We looked up in confusion. If we could only get him out of the way before the captain entered! He waited while we pondered how to answer.

"What ladies do you wish to see?" I asked.

"Well, this is good! Little madam, may I take this seat beside you?"

He dropped into the chair between us and we caught for an instant his old merry laugh, "nipped in the bud," it is true, for we gave him a warning glance. Mrs. Harris was considerate and tactful, and we not only had our corner to ourselves, but attention and observation diverted from us as much as possible. We were much amused at Captain Lock's "make-up," and he was evidently very proud of it.

"It must be very clever for your eyes not to have seen through it," he said. "I have been looking up at your window and watching you every day. I saw, too, that you made merry at my expense. It was a great temptation to speak to you many times, but I didn't want to make advances nor to ask permission to call until I knew something about how the land lay over here."

"You don't know how anxious we have been about you, or how glad and thankful we are to see you," we assured him. "We have been very uneasy at not hearing from you. Where is Mr. Holliway?"

"God knows!" he answered gravely. "He was afraid to follow my fortunes, I think. He left me at Frederick. He ought to be here by now, but if he is he is keeping very close."

"He is not here," we answered. "We have been to see his mother and sister, and they know nothing of him."

"Then something is wrong. He had an dea that we might be tracked to Frederick very easily from Berlin, and from Frederick to this place if we came by the direct route; so he branched off into West Virginia, intending to reach Baltimore by a more roundabout route than mine. Poor Holliway! he was not well, and he was nervous and unstrung over this trip from the first. He felt that I was reckless and that I was throwing away my own chance and his."

Some one in the room came near us and we returned to generalities. Very soon after Captain Locke made his adieux, promising to call again when we could arrange it.

Captain Hosmer had sought opportunities for showing special courtesies to me, but I had rather repelled him. He was good enough, however, to ignore my bad manners and to persist in turning my music for me. We had dances very often in the evenings, I playing the same tunes for folks to dance by that I played for the Prussians and that I play for my children. One night, I had the audacity to rattle off the Virginia reel, and they danced it with spirit, every Yankee of them. My fingers were just itching to play Dixie, and I don't know what foolhardiness I might have been guilty of if Captain Hosmer, who was turning my music, had not bent over me and said:

"I would like to have a little private talk with you, Miss Duncan. I know who you are. You are from the South and you have run the blockade. Your position is not free from danger. You are suspected. Pray be careful. When you have finished this, go upstairs and I will follow you."

His manner was so serious that it took all the saucy daring out of me. Perhaps it saved me from playing Dixie. As soon as I could do so without attracting observation, I got Milicent to take my place, and went up-stairs to the private parlor.

I had hardly taken my seat when he came in.

"I was sorry to attack you so suddenly," he said, "but you were so shy of me that it was my only chance."

I had learned to like and to trust him; he was honest and kind, and I told him my situation frankly. Of course I didn't explain Captain Locke.

"It is not so bad as it might be," he said, "But you must have a care about your associates. People in this house are always more or less under observation, and arrest on charge of treason is not an unknown thing in it."

"I am married." When I came to that part of my confession the captain looked surprised indeed.

"Didn't you guess from the dignity I have displayed that I was a matron?"

"I never dreamed it! I don't mean that you were not dignified," he added quickly, and in some confusion.

"My husband is a staff-officer in the rebel army," I added proudly.

"Lucky fellow!"

"I think he is a lucky fellow to be a staff-officer in the rebel army."

"To be your husband, I meant."

"I wonder if he would agree with you there!" We were on a subject very interesting to me now.

"I will show you his picture in the morning," I volunteered.

"Better not," Captain Hosmer said promptly.

I suppose I must have shown how hurt I was, for he added quickly "Of course I'll be glad to see his picture. Don't forget to bring it down at breakfast."

But he had frozen me for the time being. I could not talk

about Dan to him when I saw it bored him to listen, so we went back to the original subject of our conversation. Among other persons he spoke of Mrs. Lineman.

"I see that you are inclined to form an intimacy there. Mrs. Lineman is in perfect sympathy with the South, but, as you know, her sister is not. They do not speak now, but family differences are frequently made up. Then confidences ensue. And Mrs. Bonds is really a political spy for the North. She thinks the mystery about you is deeper than it is, and you will do well to be on your guard before her and my brothers in arms whom you meet in this house. Major Brooks already has suspicions about you."

"I don't like him," I said viciously.

"Disguise that fact a little better if you can. I don't think any of the gentlemen whom you meet here are malicious, or that they will go out of their way to harm you, but it is good policy to temper your cold civility toward them with a little more warmth."

"You are very good," I said humbly, "and I really mean to act according to your advice."

He smiled. "You are not good at playing the hypocrite, are you?"

"I must improve. But I really must tell you - I don't need to be a hypocrite with you, you know - I believe Major Brooks is malicious."

He laughed outright. "Be careful not to offend him, then. Ah, I am afraid my first lesson in diplomacy will only have skin-deep results."

The next morning I did not forget Dan's picture. I brought it down with me, and slipped it into Captain Hosmer's hand as I passed behind him to my seat at the breakfast table. I was very much pleased later when he told me what a fine fellow he thought Dan must be, and that he thought the picture very handsome. Then I talked about Dan again until he was bored - when I shut up. After this I saw a great deal of Captain Hosmer He was always so thoroughly well-bred that his attentions were very agreeable to me in spite of his uniform, and I formed a warm personal friendship and attachment for him. We were also seeing a good deal of Captain Locke.

I thought him very reckless in visiting us as he did, and I told him so frankly. He had doffed his disguise, wig and all, and appeared now every day, and sometimes oftener, at Mrs. Harris's in his own proper person, dressed in citizen's clothes. He came openly to the parlor in the daytime immediately after breakfast or lunch; and he was always there after dinner when the parlors were thronged. Several times he had joined the dance, selecting, by the way, Mrs. Bonds for a partner more than once. In fact, he singled this lady out for a number of pleasant courtesies. I could not keep him out of the way of the Yankee officers, and Major Brooks was always starting up at us somewhere like a Banquo's ghost. His eyes got sharper and sharper until I thought they would cut me in two. In halls and by-ways I was always coming upon him and always getting out of his way, and I was always surprising a cynical little grin on his face. One day I encountered him on the first landing of the stairway, squarely face to face. He addressed me, wishing me good morning gruffly, and standing in such a position that I could not pass him without rudeness unless he moved to one side. He did not move, and I was at bay.

"I know who you are, Miss Duncan," he said mischievously. "You are a good rebel now, aren't you?"

"Yes, I am a good rebel, as you call it. I'm a Virginian - and a rebel like Washington was, and like Lee is."

"I thought so. And you ran the blockade to get here."

"That's so, too. I got across at Berlin."

"I wish you'd tell me how."

I told him how. I sat down on the stairs to talk, and my enemy sat down beside me. Captain Hosmer came in, looked up, and saw the confidential and apparently friendly situation, laughed, and went on to breakfast.

"I don't call that running the blockade," he said. "I call

that storming it. I didn't think it possible to cross at Berlin or, indeed, at any other point. Our line at the Potomac has been greatly strengthened and the rules are very rigid and inspection most thorough."

"I managed to cross at Berlin because you had such a nice provost marshal there. He knew two little women couldn't do any harm."

"Humph! He doesn't know women as I do, then!"

"Perhaps he had always known only very lovely ladies," I said with the softness of a purring cat.

He grinned. "You'll be wanting to run back soon, I dare say."

"I reckon I will. I wish you'd help me. Can't you tell me how?"

He laughed outright. "You are cool!" he said.

"You know what my duty is?" he added after a pause.

"Yes," I answered. "To fight on the right side, but I'm afraid you'll never do that. Now, I have been wanting to play Dixie ever since I've been here, and I'm afraid of nobody but you. To-night I mean to play it." But I did not. That afternoon a card was brought up to Milicent and me. Major Littlebob, U. S. A., was sorry to disturb us, but would we please step down a minute. "Major Brooks came in with him," said the servant who brought the message.

"Major Brooks is going to have us arrested," I thought in terror. Milicent also was frightened by the message and by a call from an unknown officer of the United States army who came accompanied by Major Brooks. Mother followed us in fear and trembling to the parlor door as we went in to behold - Milicent's own curly-headed Bobby, all rigged out in Major Brooks's regimentals! There he was, all swallowed up in sash, sword, and hat of a United States major of infantry; beside him was the major, laughing merrily. Milicent, in her relief, bent over and kissed again and again the fairest, softest, cutest, sweetest Major Littlebob that ever wore the regimentals of the U. S. A.; and it is needless to say that after this we were never again afraid of Major Brooks.

"So, the whole purpose of your running the blockade was a visit to your mother?" Major Brooks had asked.

"And to accompany my sister. And - to buy a few things - needles, pins, and so forth," I added in confusion.

Again the major laughed at my expense. Should I confide the Confederate uniform to him and Captain Hosmer? I decided to draw the line at this, as I had drawn it at Captain Locke. Of course, Captain Locke's story was his, not mine, and the uniform - well, the uniform was Dan's, or, rather, I hoped it would be. It was never out of my mind. I would have failed in half my mission if I did not buy it and get it across the Potomac to Dan. To buy shoes, gloves, ribbons, etc., was an easy matter, but to buy a Confederate uniform in Yankeeland, that was a more delicate affair. It was Captain Locke who helped me out. He told met where I could buy it, and offered to get it for me himself, but he was taking so many risks on his own account that I was determined he should take none on mine. He directed me to a tailoring establishment on the corner of Charles and St. Paul's Streets. The head of this establishment sympathized with the South and had supplied many Southern uniforms, and his store had a convenient double entrance, one on St. Paul's and one on Charles Street. One morning I went in at the Charles Street entrance. I had chosen an early hour, and I found no one in but the tailor.

"I want to buy a Confederate uniform," I said. "Captain Locke referred me."

"Walk straight on out at the other door," he whispered. "I see two soldiers coming in from the Charles Street side."

Without looking behind me I walked straight on as if I had merely passed through the store to get to the other sidewalk. I heard some one coming rapidly behind me, and then I was joined by Captain Hosmer.

"What are you in such a hurry for?" he asked. "Wait a minute and I can walk home with you. I have a commission to execute back here."

Accordingly I returned to the store with him, was introduced to the friend accompanying him, and after a few moments walked home between the two. But the tailor had given me a hint - I was to come still earlier next day.

The next morning, however, he signaled me to pass on as I was about to enter. At last one morning I caught him alone long enough to get my uniform.

"I have to be very careful lately," he apologized for waving me off the previous day. "These Yankees suspect me and are always on the lookout. Now we will get the uniform in a hurry. I have several pieces of fine Confederate cloth just in that I will show you. Is your husband a private?"

"Oh, no-o!" I exclaimed indignantly.

"I thought not," he said suavely. "What is his rank?"

"He is a captain of cavalry now. That is - he was when I left home. But I haven't heard from him since. He may be major or colonel by now. Can't you fix up a uniform that would do for him if he is a captain or a colonel or a major when I get back, or - that would do for a general?"

"Certainly, certainly, madam. Very wise of you to think of that."

He showed me several pieces of very fine and beautiful cloth of Confederate gray, and I made my selection.

"The question is, how are you to get it across the line. In what way will you carry it?"

"Ah, that I don't know. Captain Locke advised me to consult you."

The tailor, who seemed to have had a liberal experience in such matters, considered for a moment.

"Are other ladies going with you?"

"My mother."

"It is easy then. I will cut this cloth into lengths that will be all right for the tailor who makes the uniform. You and your mother can make it into two Balmoral skirts. That's the way you get your cloth home. Now for the buttons and gold lace. Will you travel in the wrap you have on?"

"In one like it; I shall pack this in my trunk. The inspectors will not be so likely to condemn this if they find it in a trunk as they would be to condemn a new one. So I will get a new cloak South; mother will wear another."

"I see." He was impressed with the scheme and made a mental note of it. "Send me your cloaks and I'll fix the buttons all right."

Cloaks of the period were long, sacque-like affairs, double-breasted and with two rows of buttons. The tailor changed the buttons on our cloaks for Confederate brass buttons covered with wadding, and then with cloth like the wrap. The gold lace was to be folded flat and smooth. Mother was to rip the lining from the bottom of her satchel, lay the lace on the bottom, and carefully paste the lining back. We wanted to take Dan some flannel shirts, and again fashion favored us. Ladies wore wide plaid scarfs passed around their necks and falling in long ends in front. We got seven yards of fine soft flannel in a stylish plaid and cut it in two lengths. Mother, being quite tall, could wear a longer scarf than myself, so, between us, we managed to carry around our necks two good shirts for Dan.

Chapter XVI

THE FLOWER OF CHIVALRY

IN the meantime we were growing more and more uneasy about Captain Locke. We felt that he was suspected and covertly watched, but he laughed at our fears.

He and I had begun to discuss ways and means of getting back to Virginia. One day, as usual, he was sitting beside me in the parlor after dinner, and, as usual, we were talking together in low tones, and again, as usual, the parlors were full. At one end of the room sat Major Brooks and Colonel Whipple, honoring us now and then with the covert and curious observation to which I could never become hardened. Captain Hosmer was walking restlessly up and down the floor, and casting uneasy glances toward us. He was too much of a gentleman to catechize me about my friend, but I knew he was not only curious but concerned in regard to my intimacy with Captain Locke.

Captain Locke was saying to me that he was in favor of our taking some schooner going down the bay and landing somewhere in Gloucester County, when I became so painfully conscious that the eyes of the enemy were upon us that I could not attend to what he was saying.

"What is the matter with you?" he asked. "You are not thinking at all of what I am saying. I reckon your mind is on Dan Grey."

"I am thinking about you," I said, on the verge of tears. "If you are not more careful, you won't get back home at all, I'm afraid."

"Why?" he asked innocently, and as if he were the most prudent person in the world.

"Only what Milicent and I have been telling you all along. You come here openly and boldly in the presence of all these Yankees. You visit us, and we feel responsible for any misfortune that might come to you through it. It is well known now, I think, by everybody in the house that we are Southerners and blockade-runners. No one in the house except ourselves and Mrs. Harris knows who you really are. Don't you suppose people wonder?"

He had been introduced several times to ladies as Mr. Moore, but we had not introduced him generally. We did not know what to do with him. For ourselves, we felt safe by this time, but I never sat on that sofa by Captain Locke's side without the fear in my heart that a sergeant- at-arms might walk in and lay hands on his shoulder.

"Don't you see," I went on, "how Captain Hosmer is watching you?"

For Hosmer was watching him with a scrutiny which could be felt in spite of all his courteous efforts at concealment. "And can't you see with what suspicious looks those officers across the room regard you?"

"That's so. You must introduce me to some of these people."

I was dumfounded. So this was the result of my caution!

"By which of your names shall I call you?" I asked satirically, but the satire was lost on him.

"The last one. That is a good name. It is nearly as common as Smith. Besides, I really have a right to it. I came by it honestly. I have a friend in New York by that name and he has kindly lent it to me for emergencies. So if anybody wants to write or telegraph to New York about it, they will find me all right. My cousin in New York - who really is my cousin many degrees removed - will acknowledge me. He is well known in business circles there."

"Whom shall I introduce you to?"

"I would rather meet those officers."

"Good gracious!"

He smiled. "They can give me more, and more accurate, information than anybody else, and of just the kind I want."

"You are going to get yourself shot before you start home. I won't be responsible for you."

"They don't shoot spies - they hang 'em," he said cheerfully.

I believe his cheerful ease carried us safely through this conversation under the eyes of the enemy, as it had done before.

"Those gentlemen would hardly think me entitled to the courtesy of a bullet," he went on with the utmost sang-froid. "A rope is more in accordance with my expectations if I am caught. But I do not expect to be caught. Really, little madam, the frank and open plan is the best. If I were to visit you clandestinely it would create more suspicion. Don't you see the fact that you haven't presented me to those gentlemen is in itself suspicious? Call those officers up and do the honors."

"I will call Captain Hosmer," I said faintly. "I really haven't the nerve to summon the other two. - Captain Hosmer!" I called.

He came instantly, and I saw that he was glad to be called.

"Captain Hosmer, let me introduce you to my friend, Mr. Moore."

"Mr. Moore" rose, and the two gentlemen bowed and shook hands with each other. Then they sat down, the Federal captain on one side of me, the rebel captain on the other, and we had a pleasant chat. Captain Hosmer asked "Mr. Moore" if he was related to Henry P. Moore, of New York, and "Mr. Moore" replied in the affirmative. Captain Hosmer knew this gentleman very well. Captain Locke was introduced to Major Brooks and Colonel Whipple, and it ended by Captain Locke and Schenck's adjutant walking down the street together. Captain Hosmer and I watched them from the window as they strolled past, smoking their cigars.

"Your friend is a very handsome man," he said.

"You think so? Dan is ever so much handsomer."

"No doubt of it," he laughed.

The next day I said to Captain Locke: "You - you wouldn't have to use information received from these gentlemen in any way that might ever hurt them, would you? We wouldn't have to do that, would we?"

"Dear little madam, it is not probable that they will honor me with too much confidence No hurt could ever come to one who is kind to you through me. My first duty is to the South; so is yours. But honor between man and man is honor, and friendship is friendship, even in war times. In my life it has sometimes been very hard to know the line."

And there rested on his face at this moment the nearest thing to a shadow that I had ever seen there.

"I don't want you to think I have been reckless of your safety in coming here to see you. I am quite sure of my ground. You are not involved in any of my operations. And if anything were to happen, I have friends here who could extricate you even if they could not save me. The principal thing I wish to find out, now, from your Federal friends here is how you may get back to Virginia safely - since you will go. If I find out that my attendance on you will be to your disadvantage, little madam, we must give that up."

It was I who had shown most anxiety that we should go together. While we were talking Captain Hosmer came in, and I made room for him on the other side of me. The two men greeted each other cordially. They had taken a liking to each other, and the rebel captain said to the other:

"My friend here has just been consulting me as to the route she had best take in getting home. I suggested that you might advise her to better purpose."

"I deplore Miss Duncan's determination to go," said Captain Hosmer. "Almost any route is unsafe just now - if possible. However, I will be glad to do anything I can. Have you any plan under consideration?"

"Wait a minute, captain," I said, rising. "I will go and get a little map I have, and show you the route which Mr. Moore advised me to take."

I went out, leaving the two officers together. When I returned I resumed my seat between them, spread the map open upon my lap, and they bent over it, Federal and Confederate heads touching, while I traced the route with my finger.

"You see, Mr. Moore thinks I might go down the bay in a schooner and land somewhere here in Gloucester County."

"No! no! you mustn't go that way!" exclaimed Captain Hosmer quickly. "You are sure to be taken up if you try that. With all due deference to you, Mr. Moore, my knowledge of the position of our forces convinces me that that is impossible."

"Of course, as an officer in the army, you must be better informed than I am," Captain Locke said simply. "That is why I advised Miss Duncan to consult you."

"Your best plan is to go by Harper's Ferry. It is a difficult matter to get through anywhere now, but if you get to Virginia at all I think it must be by way of Harper's Ferry."

Major Brooks and Colonel Whipple joined us, and the matter ended as on the previous day, by Captain Locke and Colonel Whipple walking off down the street together.

"Moore is a splendid fellow," Captain Hosmer said to me, when we had the sofa to ourselves. "I am glad you introduced us. Your not doing so looked suspicious, and I was troubled for fear he would get you into some scrape or other."

Dear, generous fellow, how I hated to deceive him, and how it was on the tip of my tongue to tell him who Captain Locke was, until I remembered what his duty would be if I told him! And Captain Locke's secret was mine to keep. He had been ready to risk his life rather than leave me alone at Berlin! Then, too, poor fellow, he had such a slender chance, I thought, of getting home alive that not even an enemy would care to make it worse. I used to look at his bonnie white throat and shudder.

"God bless you," he said to me once, "for all your goodness to a poor, lonely, stray fellow! You shouldn't be afraid for me. You say your 'Hail Marys' for me, you know."

I had been telling him I was afraid for him, and he had, as usual, tried to reassure me and to laugh me out of it. He was never afraid for himself - I believe he would have stood up to be shot with a laugh on his lips. I wonder if he was laughing when they shot him - my dear, brave friend!

In the meantime we had heard that Mr. Holliway had been arrested in West Virginia, was lying in prison somewhere, and that his friends were trying to get him out, and before I left Baltimore we heard that he had died in prison just as an exchange had been arranged.

My return to Virginia was the subject of daily discussions between me and my two captains, and in this way Captain Locke continued to find out ways that he must not go, and eventually that we must not go together. It was he who first said it.

"I should be no earthly good, but a disadvantage to you, little madam. Hosmer is going to see you through this thing all right."

Then, seeing my downcast look, he went on cheerily: "I'll get through somehow all or later, and we'll meet in Old Virginia. Don't bother your dear little head about me."

Captain Hosmer tried in vain to dissuade me from going. He felt that the journey under present conditions would be uncomfortable and unsafe, and that it was in every way advisable for me to stay where I was. But I was beginning to be very uneasy about Dan. I had heard from him only once since reaching Baltimore. Then his letters came in a batch, and I received them through the kindly agency of Mr. Cridland, British consul at Richmond, who had been my father's personal friend and frequent guest, and who had dandled a small person named "Nell" on his knee many times. Captain Hosmer still insisted that I must go by Harper's Ferry if I went at all, and he said that a pass was necessary.

"How on earth am I to get it?" I asked.

"I must arrange that for you," he said.

I think one reason that Captain Hosmer was so good to me was because his wife was a Southern woman. Her parents were Southern, her brothers were in the Southern army, and her husband was a Federal officer. They loved each other, but somehow they were separated, she living South with her parents. Under the pressure of the times there was a sectional conscience, and people did things which they did not wish to do, because they thought it was right. I don't know what I should have done then if I had been situated as Mrs. Hosmer was, but I know that at the present time I should stick to Dan, no matter what flag he fought under.

Perhaps we are not as great or good in peace as in war times.

The captain had a beautiful country-seat several miles out of town. We had heard much of this place and its old-time hospitalities; and we also heard that it had been virtually closed since Captain Hosmer's separation from his wife. The captain went there frequently alone, and occasionally with a few friends, but the place had known no festivity since its mistress had gone away on that visit from which, by the way, she returned before we left Baltimore.

But before she came back there was a stag party at the captain's country place, given in honor of General Fish, the provost marshal at Baltimore, and other prominent officers.

The next time I saw Captain Hosmer he had a smile for me.

"You will get your passes," he said. "I have spoken to General Fish for them."

Milicent had decided that she could not risk little Bobby on such a journey and at this season, but mother was to go with me . The day before we were to start she and I went down to General Fish's office. He was out, but an orderly told us rather rudely to sit down and wait, which invitation or command we humbly acted upon. Presently General Fish entered. We stated our case.

"We are Southerners, general, and we wish to go south by way of Harper's Ferry." "Mrs. and Miss Duncan, I think you said?"

"Yes, general."

"You are the ladies I heard of from Captain Hosmer, then?"

We gave him a note from Captain Hosmer.

"Excuse me, ladies, while I read this, and I will see what I can do for you."

He finished the note and then said:

"That's all right. I will make out your passes, ladies," and in a few minutes the important papers were in our hands.

"These will take you to General Kelly at Harper's Ferry. There my power ends. You will find General Kelly courteous and considerate, though I make no promises for him, understand. I will furnish you an escort to Harper's Ferry, and an officer will be sent to your boarding-house this afternoon to examine your baggage. Your address, please." He wrote a few words rapidly, and called the orderly:

"Take that order," he said.

The orderly saluted and got as far as the door, then he turned.

"Do these women go?" he asked of the general.

"These ladies go. Obey my order, sir!"

Upon which the orderly went quickly about his business.

When the officer came to examine our baggage I was on thorns. I had come north intending to make certain purchases, and I had made them, and the fruit of my money and labors was in those two trunks of mother's and mine. Mother's trunk was quite a large one, and both of those honest-looking trunks to which I yielded the keys so freely were crammed with dishonest goods - that is, dishonest according to blockade law. I had paid good gold for them, and anxiety enough, Heaven knows, for them to be properly mine. I had shoes in the bottom of those trunks, and on top of the shoes cloth made into the semblance of female wear and underwear; and, lastly, I had put in genuine every-day garments. There were handkerchiefs, pins, needles, gloves, thread, and all sorts of odds and ends between the folds of garments, here, there, and everywhere in those trunks. They were as contraband trunks as ever crossed into Dixie. But, again, my Yankee was a gentleman.

"This is an unpleasant duty, miss," he said when I handed him my keys, "but I will disarrange your property as little as possible. It is only a form."

The orderly lifted the trays and set them back again, scarcely glancing underneath. What a dear, nice Yankee, I thought! He locked the trunks and sealed them.

"Will those seals be broken anywhere, and my trunks examined again?" I asked in some trepidation - this examination was so satisfactory to me that I wanted it to do for one and all.

"I can not tell, miss. They may be at Harpers Ferry. But I hardly think so. I think this seal will carry you through."

Chapter XVII

PRISONERS OF THE UNITED STATES

THE officer who had examined our trunks the previous day took the trunks to the depot in a wagon, mother and I going in a hack. After we got on the train, our officer, Lieutenant Martin, joined us, and made himself very agreeable. The beginning of that journey was most pleasant. The scenery along the road to Harper's Ferry is at all times beautiful, and as we drew nearer to the ferry our car ran by the side of the Potomac, so that from one window we looked across the river to the Virginia Heights, and from the other to the Heights of Maryland. It was afternoon and growing dark when we reached Harper's Ferry.

There we found something like a riot going on, shouting and noises of all sorts, and the town full of drunken soldiers. We were told that there had been fighting in the valley, that the Federals had won, and that the men had just been paid off, and were celebrating victory and enjoying pay and booty in regular soldier fashion. Through this shouting rowdy mob mother and I passed under our Federal escort to the tavern.

When we reached the tavern, a miserable little place full of drunken soldiers, our kind escort told us that his duty was at an end, and that he must take the return train to Baltimore. I think he hated to leave us under such unsafe circumstances, but he scarcely had time to settle us in the reception-room, shake hands, and catch his train. Here mother and I sat, debating what we should do. Of course, we were extremely anxious to get out of the place. We called a waiter and asked him if he could tell us where we could hire a vehicle to take us a part of our journey, or the whole of it. He knew of nothing that we could get. Then we went out on the porch, disagreeable as this was, and made inquiries of everybody who seemed sober enough to answer, but to no purpose. We could find no way of getting out of Harper's Ferry that night.

Thoroughly frightened, we asked to be shown to the commanding officer of the place, and were ushered into General Kelly's office, which, fortunately, was attached to the tavern - really a part of it.

General Kelly rose when we entered, saw us seated, and was as courteous as possible, while we stated the case and asked his advice He heard us patiently, and was very sympathetic.

"I don't know what to say, ladies. I have no authority to send you on."

"Then what will we do, general?"

"I can not say. I can, of course, give you passes, but you will find it impossible to hire anything here to travel in just now. The best you could get would be an ox-cart or a broken-down wagon, and the roads are almost impassable for good strong vehicles. And, besides, it is not safe for you to travel except under military escort, which, as I have said, I have no authority to furnish. There has been a great deal of fighting in the valley, and the roads are lined with stragglers If you were prisoners now I could put you under escort and send you through our lines easy enough, but as it is I don't see what I can do."

We felt inclined to cry.

"And this is not a fit place for you to spend the night in, as you can see for yourselves," he pursued, very much in the manner of a Job's comforter. "The tavern is thronged with drunken men, and the whole town is overrun with them."

"Would it not be best for us to return to Baltimore?" we asked humbly. We had almost made up our minds to going back.

"That would be best, certainly - if you can."

"Why, can't we go back? We had no idea that we wouldn't be allowed to go back if we wanted to."

"Well, you see, ladies, you are in the position of Southerners sent south. The policy of the Government encourages the sending of all Southerners in Maryland south to stay. I am only explaining, that you may understand that it may be difficult for me to assist you, in spite of my willingness to do so. I can not send you back without authority from General Fish. I will telegraph to him at once, and do my best for you. My orderly will see you back to the tavern. And I will notify you when I hear from General Fish."

So we returned to the reception-room of the tavern. Among the groups thronging the tavern were a few graycoats who had been captured the day before. One of these prisoners, a tall, handsome man, walked restlessly up and down the room where we sat, his guard keeping watch on him. As he passed back and forth I looked at him sorrowfully, putting into my eyes all the sympathy and encouragement I dared.

There was something in his look when he returned mine that made me think he wanted to speak to me. Every time he passed I thought I saw his eyes growing more and more wistful under their drooping lids.

Without seeming to notice him I moved about the room until I got to a window which was in the line of his restless beat. I stood there, my back turned to him, apparently looking out of the window, until I disarmed the suspicion of the guard. Then I settled down into a seat, my side to the window, my back to the guard, my face to the prisoner when the turn in his beat brought him toward me. A swift glance showed him that I was on the alert. Not a muscle of his face changed - he was facing the guard - but when he turned and came back, as he passed me he dropped these words.

"Going south?"

He walked to the end of the room and turned. Coming back, he faced me and the guard. As he passed I said:

"Yes."

When he came back, he said - always with his head drooped and speaking below his breath and so that his lips could hardly be seen to move:

"Take a message?"

When he passed back I said:

"Yes."

Returning: "Get word to Governor Vance of North Carolina."

To the end of his beat, turning and passing again in silence, then as he walked with his back to the guard:

"You saw Charlie Vance here - "

To the end of beat one way, to the end another, and back again:

"Prisoner - captured in fight yesterday."

Several beats back and forth in silence, then:

"Carried north."

Again:

"Don't know where."

This was the last he had opportunity to say. I saw the orderly coming in. Before Lieutenant Vance was near enough to catch another word from me, the orderly stood before me, a telegram in his hand. It was from General Fish to General Kelly:

"The ladies were sent south at their own request. I decline further connection with the matter."

"Why - why," I cried in desperation, "we can't go south, we can't go north, and we can't stay here!"

There was a pert little Yankee in the room who had been watching us for some time. He, like everybody else around us, understood by this time our dilemma.

"I'll tell you how to get sent on, if you will listen," he said.

"I will," I said clearly and firmly, and looking straight into the eyes of Lieutenant Vance, who was then passing close by me.

The little Yankee was staggered by the unnecessary amount of resolution expressed in my reply. I kept my eyes focused on the spot where Mr. Vance had been for some seconds after he had passed. Then I turned to my little Yankee. I had snubbed him severely heretofore, but I was humbled by extremity, and willing enough now to listen if he could tell us how to get away from this place.

"Tell us how we can get sent on," I asked.

"Just step out there in the street and holler for Jeff Davis, and you'll get sent on quick enough!"

We withered him with a stare, and then turned our backs on him, and at the same moment two ladies entered the room whom we recognized. They were Mrs. Drummond and Miss Oglesby, whose acquaintance we had made in Baltimore, and they, too, were going south. They explained that they had been in this wretched place since yesterday, and that they were not allowed to return to Baltimore and were unable to go home. They had been out trying to find a conveyance of some sort, but had been able to secure only the promise of an ox-cart, and hearing that we were here had come in to consult with us. During all this time the orderly, whom I had detained, was waiting impatiently. We decided to go with him and make another appeal to General Kelly. Accordingly the whole party filed into General Kelly's office again.

"What are we to do, general?" I cried out in desperation. "We can't go back, we can't go on, and we can't stay here!"

The kindly general did honor to the stars he wore - he was a gentleman, every inch of him. It happened later that he was captured and held in Libby Prison in Richmond, and I was in Richmond and didn't know it. I have held a grudge against fate ever since. If I had only known, he would have been reminded by every courtesy that a Southern woman could render of how gratefully his kindness was remembered.

"I hardly hoped for a different answer from General Fish, ladies. The regulations on this point are very stringent. And I can not return you to Baltimore unless you take the oath of allegiance."

"What?" we asked eagerly.

"If you take the oath of allegiance, I can send you back."

We decided to do this.

We didn't know exactly what the oath was, but we thought we could take anything to get us out of our scrape. We told General Kelly we would take it, and we were conducted into another room, which I can only remember as being full of Federal soldiers. We were marched up to a desk where a man began reading the oath to us. It was the famous "ironclad." We did not wait for him to get through. Without a word each of us turned and marched back into General Kelly's office, as indignant a set of women as could be found.

He was looking for us - doubtless he knew by previous experience the effect the reading of that oath produced upon Southern women - and he burst out laughing as our procession filed back into his room.

"Why, general," we began, "we couldn't take that horrid thing! We are Southerners, and our kinsmen and friends are Southern soldiers."

"I almost knew you wouldn't take that oath, ladies, when I sent you there."

"General," I said, "this is the most remarkable position I ever knew people to be in - where you can't go back, and can't go forward, and can't stay where you are. I don't know what you are to do with us, general, unless you hang us to get us out of the way."

He laughed heartily.

"I must do something a little better than that for you. My orderly will take you back to the tavern, and you will hear from me in an hour."

We went with Mrs. Drummond and Miss Oglesby to their room. Before the hour was up we were escorted to another interview with General Kelly. The general beamed on us.

"Here is a telegram I received in your absence," he said, handing it to us:

"Mrs. and Miss Duncan are dear friends of mine. Can you see them through? If not, tell them I will be in Harper's Ferry to-night. Answer.

"HOSMER."

"Here is my answer," said the general:

"Stay where you are. Will see them through all right."

"KELLY."

"How could he have found out the trouble we were in?" we asked in wonder.

"I don't know. News of the fighting in the valley and the conditions of things here reached Baltimore soon after you left there. Hosmer perhaps got an idea of your situation through General Fish. He may have gone to Fish's office to inquire. Hosmer is a capital fellow and an old friend of mine. I had about determined on what to do for you before I heard from him, but I thought it would please you to know of his message. I will ask you to return to the tavern, ladies, and exercise a little further patience. You will hear from me soon."

This time we waited only a little while before an orderly rapped at the door to say that an ambulance was in waiting for us below. We hurried down with him, and in ten minutes were inside the ambulance, and prisoners of the United States.

Behind us into the ambulance stepped a dashing young officer, all brass buttons and gold lace.

"I am Captain Goldsborough," he said, saluting, "commissioned by General Kelly to attend you."

Our escort consisted of five soldiers who followed us, sitting in a wagon on our baggage. That afternoon we passed through Charlestown, and there Captain Goldsborough pointed out to us the house in which John Brown had lived - an ordinary two-story frame house.

As well as I can remember we reached Berryville about nine o'clock. Our ambulance drew up in front of the tavern, and Captain Goldsborough went in to see about getting accommodations for us. He came out quickly and said, "This is no fit place tonight for you, ladies. I am informed that there is an old couple on the hill who may take us in. I hear, too, that they are good Confederates," he added mischievously. Of course lights were out and everybody asleep when we drove up, but our driver went in and beat on the door until he waked the old people up. They received us kindly, and the old lady got a supper for us of cold meats and slices of loaf bread, butter, milk, preserves, and hot coffee which she must have made herself as no servants were in the house at that hour; and we had a comfortable room with two beds in it. The old lady came in and chatted with us awhile, telling us all she knew about our army's movements, and listening eagerly to what people in Maryland had to say about the war. We were very tired, but I am sure it must have been one o'clock when we went to sleep. At daybreak there came a great banging at the front door. Mother put her head out of the front window and inquired who was trying to break the door down.

It was our driver, and there at the gate stood our ambulance. The driver hurried us desperately, saying we had not a moment to lose. The noise had aroused our hosts, and when we got down the old lady had spread us a cold lunch and made us a cup of coffee.

"I was hoping to have you a nice hot breakfast," she said, "but since you must go in such a hurry this is the best I can do. If I had known you were going to make such an early start I would have got you a hot breakfast somehow."

We swallowed our food hurriedly, but this did not satisfy our driver. Every few minutes he came down on the door with the butt end of his whip. Finally we left off eating, ran upstairs, and gathered up our bags. As we hurried down, almost falling over each other in our haste, we saw a magnificent-looking soldier standing in the hall. He was in the full uniform of a colonel of cavalry, glittering with gold lace, with gauntlets reaching his elbows, and high military boots.

"Mrs. Duncan and Miss Duncan, I suppose," he said with

a sweeping bow, "and"

"Mrs. Drummond and Miss Oglesby," we said of the ladies who came behind us.

"I am Colonel McReynolds, commandant at this place, and at your service, ladies," he continued. "I have to apologize for not paying my respects to you last night upon receipt of General Kelly's letter asking me to take charge of you. The lateness of the hour must be my excuse. At the time Captain Goldsborough presented it I had a number of important despatches to attend to, and I supposed you were tired out and in need of rest."

We expressed our appreciation of his courtesy and General Kelly's thoughtfulness.

"What is all this?" he asked, pointing to our ambulance, baggage wagon, and impatient driver.

We explained that they were the conveniences furnished us by General Kelly.

"But you surely do not propose starting off in such weather as this, ladies?"

I have neglected to say that it had been storming since daybreak.

"The driver has been beating on the doors since before day," somebody said.

"He has, has he? Then he has exceeded his instructions. He had no right whatever to disturb you, ladies. I will see that he is reported."

He called the driver and reprimanded him sharply.

"Pray don't feel that you must leave us in such weather as this, ladies," he continued with the utmost kindness. "Stay here a week if you like. That ambulance and wagon and those men and horses are at your service as long as you choose to keep them here, and we will be glad to do whatever we may for your comfort or pleasure until it suits your own convenience to leave us."

We hardly knew how to thank this princely young enemy, but we insisted that the driver should not be punished, and that we should be allowed to proceed on our journey, as we were anxious to rcach our friends and kindred.

He rode in our ambulance with us to his headquarters, where we were joined by our other charming enemy, and, making our adieux to the gallant and handsome colonel, continued our journey.

During the day something happened to Captain Goldsborough's watch, and it stopped running, much to his annoyance.

"I should like to know what time it is," he said.

I pulled my watch out and held it open for him to see the time. I could have told him what hour it was. I don't know what made me such a reckless little creature in those days. The watch I held to him had a tiny Confederate flag pasted inside. My companions had either secreted their watches or were not traveling with them. I had been urged to do the same, but had openly worn my watch ever since leaving Baltimore. Captain Goldsborough saw the hour, and he saw the flag also. He stared at me in utter amazement.

"You are brave - or reckless," he said.

"I know this is contraband goods, and, according to your ideas, treasonable. Will you confiscate it?" quietly holding it out again.

His face flushed.

"Not I! but some one else might. You are not prudent to wear that openly."

And I was so ashamed of myself for hurting his feelings that I made amends in rather too warm terms, I am afraid, considering that he didn't know I was married and a privileged character.

"You are traveling in the wrong direction, I think, Miss Duncan," he ventured to say after awhile. "You shouldn't leave the North and go south now."

"Why?"

"I - I shouldn't think you would receive the attention there just now that is your due. You are young and fond of society, I imagine. And - there are so few beaux in the South now - I shouldn't think you would like that."

"Really?"

"I mean that I wish you would stay up North where it is pleasanter. It's so - uncomfortable down South. You are so young, you see, you ought to have a chance to enjoy life a little. I - I wish you were up here - and I could add a little to your happiness. I - I mean," catching a glance which warned him, "it is must be dull for you in the South - no beaux - no nothing."

"All the beaux are in the field," I retorted, "where they ought to be. I wouldn't have a beau who wasn't, and if I were a Northern girl I wouldn't have a man who didn't wear a uniform - though, I think, it ought to be gray."

"I expect you have a sweetheart down South whom you expect to see when you get home. That is why your heart has been so set on getting back."

"If I had a sweetheart down South I couldn't see him when I got back home, for he would be in the field."

"So, your sweetheart is a Southern soldier?" wistfully.

"I wouldn't have a sweetheart who wasn't a soldier - a Southern soldier."

In the other side of my watch I had pasted a small picture of Dan in uniform. I opened this side and held it out to my companion.

"That's my sweetheart's picture."

He looked at it long and hard. "A good-looking fellow," he said, "and I have no doubt a gallant soldier. If I ever meet him in battle - he will be safe from my bullet."

Behind our wagon all the way from Harper's Ferry had come a party equipped like ourselves. They were Jews, and, as we were informed, were prisoners of the United States. They had an ambulance like ours, a baggage wagon like ours, and a similar escort of five infantry perched on trunks. Their escort who rode inside, however, was not so attractive as ours. We felt and expressed much commiseration for them because they were prisoners - "those poor Jews," we called them.

We were all suffering the consequences of late and early hours, and of the worry and excitement at Harper's Ferry. I felt almost ill, and when Miss Oglesby, whose home was in Winchester, invited us to spend a week with her, we concluded that we would accept her hospitality until better able to continue our journey.

Winchester was the most difficult of all places for Southerners to pass through at this time, and we could not possibly have gotten through if we had been left to our own resources. Milroy was commandant, and his name was a terror. He belonged to the Ben Butler of New Orleans type. Some time near the middle of the day we drew up in front of Milroy's headquarters. Immediately behind us came the Jews and their belongings. They did not go in with us, and I supposed they were awaiting their turn. General Milroy was absent, off on a fight, and we fell into the hands of his adjutant, a dapper little fellow. We heard him talking to Goldsborough of the recent fight and victory, and heard him making arrangements for our transportation.

Here we thought it proper to inform him that we were going to remain a week in Winchester.

"You can not remain here," he said. "You go on immediately."

"Oh, no!" we said, "we're not going on now. We are going to stop here for a visit and until we are rested."

"You are prisoners and under orders. You go at once," he began bruskly.

"Oh, no!" we interrupted, eager to enlighten him, for we saw he had made a very natural mistake. "We are not prisoners. Those poor Jews out there, they are prisoners. We are going to stop here on a little visit."

"You don't stop here an hour. This is Miss Oglesby's destination, and she stops, but the rest of you go on - now."

He looked as if he thought us demented. Goldsborough kept making faces at us, but we were so anxious to correct the adjutant's mistake that we had no attention to bestow elsewhere. We thought we had never seen so stupid a man as that adjutant.

"We are not the prisoners," we insisted. "Those Jews out there."

Here he told Captain Goldsborough to conduct "these prisoners" down-stairs and into the ambulance provided for them. "You will not go far before you meet a detachment of cavalry on their way to this place," he informed Captain Goldsborough, and then instructed him to turn back of these a sufficient escort for our party.

We were in a perfect rage as Captain Goldsborough led us down-stairs. We thought Milroy's adjutant the very rudest and stupidest person we had ever seen.

Chapter XVIII

Within Our Lines

AFTER leaving the saucy and peremptory adjutant we were shown into the handsomest ambulance I have ever seen. I suppose the one we had been using was returned to Harper's Ferry or left at Winchester for the horses to rest until Captain Goldsborough's return. At any rate, we were in new quarters, and very elegant ones they were. The sides and seats were cushioned and padded, and it was really a luxurious coach. It was drawn by four large black horses with coats like silk. There was a postilion on the seat, and beside him sat a small boy who kept peeping behind us and into the woods on all sides, and as far ahead as possible. I didn't know what he was trying to see or find out, but I came to the conclusion that he was there to "peep" on general principles.

As soon as we were seated we asked Captain Goldsborough what upon earth that impertinent adjutant meant by referring to us as "prisoners," and ordering us about so.

Whereupon he explained with much embarrassment and many apologies that we were really prisoners - that General Kelly could not have sent us through without the formality of putting us under arrest.

"I wish," he said in an aside to me, "that I didn't have to release you."

Of course we were perfectly satisfied to be General Kelly's prisoners under such circumstances. In fact, we charged Captain Goldsborough to tell him how nice we thought it was to be put under arrest by him.

We withdrew our charges against the adjutant, and even acknowledged that there was kindness in the pert little Yankee's telling us to "holler for Jeff Davis and we'd get sent on quick enough."

Six miles from Winchester we met the detachment of cavalry to which Milroy's adjutant had referred. It was a magnificent-looking body of men, handsomely uniformed and mounted. As they were about to dash past us Captain Goldsborough halted them, gave an order, and instantly thirty riders wheeled out of line and surrounded the ambulance, the others riding on without a break in their movements. Captain Goldsborough had gotten out of the ambulance some minutes before we met the detachment of cavalry, and was sitting with the driver, having sent the little boy inside. It sounds rather a formidable position for a Southern woman, a blockade-runner, in a Yankee ambulance, and surrounded by thirty Yankees armed to the teeth; but I was never safer in my life. The little boy was in a state of terror that would have been amusing if it had not been pitiful.

"What are all these men around the ambulance for?" I asked. He didn't look as if he could get his wits together at once.

"Are they afraid we will get away?" I continued.

"Oh, no'm! no'm!" he answered, his eyes as big as saucers. "There's been lots of fightin' - an' there's rebels all along here in the woods - and they'd come out and take this here ambulance an' these here horses - an' we all, an' you all, an' all of us!"

A novel position, truly, Yankees protecting us against our own soldiers! We met another company of soldiers, and alas! we could turn back none of them. They were not mounted, they were not handsomely uniformed. From the windows of our ambulance we looked out on them with tearful eyes, and waved our handkerchiefs to them; but their heads were bowed, and they did not see us. They would hardly have believed we were prisoners if they had seen us, for our escort of Union cavalry the whole time they guarded us treated us as if we were quccns. Not one profane word did we hear - not a syllable that breathed anything but respect and kindly feeling.

At Newtown we were released and were Union prisoners no longer, but Southern travelers close to the Southern lines and on our own responsibility. Captain Goldsborough bade us adieu, saying that he was sorry he could not take us farther, but that his orders compelled him to turn back here, and we poured out our gratitude to him and to Colonel McReynolds and General Kelly by him. He put a little sentiment into a farewell pressure of my hand, and I am afraid I put a great deal too much gratitude and penitence into my eyes. My genius for friendship had asserted itself, and I was fast learning to give him a companion niche in my heart with Captains Hosmer and Locke. Another day with him, and I would have told him I was married, showed him Dan's picture, bored him with Dan, and found in him all the better friend and good comrade.

Our hearts sank as our gallant bluecoat, our cozy ambulance, and our cavalry guard left us, three lonely women in the tavern at Newtown. We spent the night there, and the next morning secured, with much difficulty, a small, uncovered, one-horse wagon to take us on our journey. We were very much crowded. Our trunks were piled up in it - mother's, Mrs. Drummond's, and my own. I made mother as comfortable as possible, and Mrs. Drummond carefully made herself so, while I sat on the seat with the driver, a trunk sticking in my back all the way. I had to sit almost double because of the trunk, the wagon being so small that no other arrangement was possible.

Rain had fallen plentifully here. The day was one of fogs and mists with occasional light showers, the roads were muddy and seamed with ruts, over which the wagon jogged up and down, and I jogged with it, feeling as if my back would break in two and almost wishing it would and end my misery. About nine of that miserable wet night we hailed with eager, glad, tired hearts and eyes the lights of Woodstock. Here we knew we should find Southern forces encamped, here we knew we should be at home among our own people. Just outside the town a voice rang through the darkness:

"Halt!"

A sentry stood in our path.

"We are Southerners," we said. "Let us pass."

"Where are your papers?"

"Papers? We haven't any papers. We are Southerners, we tell you - Southern ladies, and we are in a hurry, and you must let us pass right now."

"I can't do it. Show your papers or turn back."

We set up a wail.

"Here, we've come all the way from Baltimore, and the Yankees have sent us and have brought us all the way in a fine ambulance and cavalry escorts and big horses and gold lace and everything, and now we've got home, and our own people won't let us in! tell us to turn back!"

The sentry seemed impressed. Rags and musket, he was a pathetic if stern figure as he stood in that lonely, muddy road in the glare of our driver's lantern.

But he was firm. He told us that he was obeying orders and could not let us by since we had no passes.

"I'm so tired, and my back is almost broken with this trunk sticking into it," I moaned.

"That ain't comfortable," he admitted, but his resolute position in the middle of the road showed that we couldn't pass, all the same.

"Look here," I said, plucking up some of my accustomed spirit, "do you know that my husband is an officer in the Confederate army? My husband is Captain Grey."

"Can't help it. Got to obey orders."

"And my brother," said Mrs. Drummond, "is a colonel in the Confederate army. To think that I - I, the sister of Colonel am told that I can't pass here!"

"Law, ma'am! that's my colonel!" said the man. "I tell

you what I'll do, ladies. I'll send a note in to the colonel and see what he says about it."

So we waited till he found a passer-by who would be a messenger; and then we waited until the messenger replied to the note, and we were permitted to pass.

Soon after we reached the tavern the news of our arrival and exploits got abroad and soon the little tavern parlor was filled with people listening to the tales of the blockade-runners who were just from Yankeeland, bringing a trunk or two full of clothes. The news of our doughty deeds spread from house to house, and soldiers gathered in front of the tavern and gave us ringing cheers, and welcomed us home with all their lung power. Poor, ragged fellows! how I did wish that mother and I had worn home a hundred or two more Balmorals!

The next morning we left Woodstock.

We were traveling now in a comfortable spring wagon, and made good time, reaching Harrisonburg in time to take the train for Staunton.

As we sat in the parlor of the hotel in Staunton who should walk in but an old friend and cousin of Dan's, Lieutenant Nelson! But he could tell me nothing about Dan - he did not even know where he could be found. This was just before the second battle of the Wilderness, and the cavalry was being shifted constantly from place to place. But if Lieutenant Nelson could tell us nothing, he was greatly interested in our exploits. He told him of the Balmorals with pride.

"And here are two shirts for Dan," I said, pulling at our long scarfs. "Just think of our getting through with a full uniform - cloth, brass buttons, gold lace, and all!"

As at Woodstock, the story of our prowess spread. It went from one person to another until the soldiers got hold of it, and gathered around the hotel and more ringing cheers were given us.

The next morning we took the train for Richmond - but we did not get there.

At Lindseys Station, just before we reached Gordonsville, a man in the uniform of the Thirteenth got on.

I called him to me.

"Can you tell me where the Thirteenth is?"

"Yes'm. We lef' 'em 'bout the aige of Culpeper, yistiddy. Lor'm! we've had times!"

"What was the matter?"

"We been havin' a heap o' fightin'. The kurnel, he warn't thar at Beverly Ford, an' we didn't have but one squadron, an' the adjutant, he led the charge an' he sholy come mighty nigh gittin' killed. Lor'm! what's the matter with ye?"

"Nothing! Go on! Make haste, tell me - make haste. The adjutant."

"His horse got shot under him, an' his courier ridin' right 'longside o' him got killed, an' the adjutant warn't hurt, not a mite But, Lortm! that was sholy a narrer escape! An' they say that the adjutant'll git promoted."

Didn't I say so? Didn't I think of that when I got the uniform?

"Thank you," I said to the man. "You bring me the first news I have had of my husband for a long time."

"Good gracious! you ain't our adjutant's wife?"

"Yes, I am. And I am glad to meet one of his soldiers. And you are the first to tell me good news."

"Lor'm, now, ain't I proud o' that! An' you our adjutant's wife. You don't say! An' I jes been a-tellin' you how it was a'mos' a mi-racle that you warn's a widder 'omen! An' you never let on! But I see you changed your face, marm, when I tole 'bout his pretty nigh gitting shot. Yes, marm; the adjutant charged beautiful! he jes rid right squar into 'em, an' he made the Yankees git!"

"How long do you think the Thirteenth will remain in Culpeper?"

"That I couldn't say for certain, marm. They mought be thar for a day or two, an' they mought be thar longer. You can't always tell much 'bout what the cavalry gwine to do.

But we's sho proud o' the adjutant, marm. Ginral Lee an' Ginral Stuart an' Kunnel Chambliss all give him the praise."

It was after this battle that Dan was promoted to the rank of major, "for gallant conduct."

I bade the soldier a hurried good-by and went to the conductor.

"My husband's regiment is in Culpeper," I said; "I have just heard it from one of his men, and I want you to put me off at Gordonsville. I have decided not to go on to Richmond, but to take the next train to Culpeper."

"The next train to Culpeper, ma'am - I think the next train for Culpeper passes Gordonsville at four in the afternoon. There's no train before that, I know, and I am not sure that there's one at four. There's no tavern nor anything to put you down at - I'll just have to set you out on the roadside."

And it was on a red roadside that we and our baggage were set down, on a bank of red mud, and there sat we on top of them as the train rolled away. The conductor left us regretfully.

"Maybe you might get accommodations at that house up there, ma'am," he had said, pointing to the only house in sight, a two-story white dwelling about a quarter of a mile distant. "I don't know what else you'll do if that train don't come along at four."

This was ten o'clock in the morning. Four o'clock came, but no train. We waited faithfully for it, but it did not come at all. At last we gave up hope and paid a boy to carry our trunks to the house on the hill. I shall never forget our reception at that house. At first they refused to take us at all. After arguing the point with them and placing our necessities before them, and promising to pay them anything they might wish; we were thankful to get a gruff:

"Come in."

We were shown to a room and shut in like horses. There was not even a fire made for us. We had been warmer sitting on the roadside in the sunshine. I will pass over the supper in silence. We had had no dinner and were hungry, and we ate for our part of that supper the upper crust of a biscuit each. A hard bed, the upper crusts of two biscuits, no fire - this was what we got at that house. The next morning we left before breakfast and went back to our mudbank in the sun, first asking for our bill and paying it. It was two dollars apiece in gold!

The train came along early, however, and we were on it, and off to Culpeper, all our troubles forgotten, for every mile was bringing us nearer to Dan. As soon as we got off I saw quite a number of soldiers belonging to Dan's command. Many of them were known to me personally. They came up and welcomed me back to Dixie, and congratulated me on my husband's gallantry and probable promotion, and I sent word to Dan by them that I was there.

He came - the raggedest, most widowed-looking officer! But weren't we happy!

"Oh, Dan! " I cried, after the first rapture of greeting, "I got it so it would do for a captain or a major or a colonel or a general. Didn't I do right?"

"What are you talking about, Nell? Got what?"

He looked as if he feared recent adventures had unsettled my intellect.

"Your uniform, Dan," I answered, but my countenance fell.

"My - uniform."

Just like a man! He had forgotten the principal thing - next to seeing mother, of course that I had gone to Baltimore for.

"Your uniform, Dan. I've got it on. Here it is," and I lifted my skirt and showed him my Balmoral. "Isn't it a beautiful cloth? And I have kept it just as nice - not a fleck of mud on it. And here are the buttons on my cloak, and I have the gold lace in mother's satchel, and."

"Nell, dear, I haven't time to talk about uniforms now. You will sleep here to-night. To-morrow I will try to get a room for you at Mr. Bradford's. I will come in the morning or send you word what to do. I am so sorry to go, but I can't stay a minute longer. Good-by, my darling."

I was waked the next morning by a voice under my window calling:

"Miss Nell! O Miss Nell!" and looking out I saw Dan's body-servant, Sam, successor to poor Josh, who had died of smallpox.

"Mars Dan say, I fotch his love to you, an' tell you you git right on dem nex' kyars an' go straight on ter Orange Court-house, case dar's too much fightin' 'roun' here. An' he gwine notify you afar when you kin come back. But he say dat if you hear dar's fight in' 'roun' Orange Court-house, den you go straight on ter Richmond, an' don't you stop untwell you git dar."

"But I don't want to go, Sam."

"But Mars Dan he say tell you p'intedly you mus'."

"Ain't he coming to tell me good-by, Sam?"

"Law, Miss Nell! how he gwine do dat when de Yankees is er-overrunnin' de whole yuth? What's guine ter become uv de country ef de major leave off fitten de Yankees to humorfy you?"

I could not for the life of me, sad as my heart was, keep from laughing at being taken to task by Sam.

"Is it so bad as that, Sam?"

"Yes'm, dat 'tis! Mars Dan say he 'fraid de Yankees git in de town hyer fo' night. De Yankees is er pressin' we all close."

"I can't see your master at all before I go, Sam?"

"Law, Miss Nell; ain't I done tole you I dat? De country will go to de dawgs ef de major stop fitten de Yankees to humorfy you."

"If your master gets hurt, Sam, will you get me word?"

"Law, yes, Miss Nell! I sholy will."

"And you'll take care of him, Sam?"

"Dat's jes what I gwine to do, Miss Nell. Me lef' de major

ef he git hu't! shuh!"

"Good-by, Sam. Tell your master I'm gone."

"Yes'm. He'll sho be p'intedly glad ter heah dat!"

Just fifteen minutes in which to catch the train. We threw things pell-mell into our trunks - there was no vehicle to be had - paid a man to drag them to the depot, and were on our way to Orange in less than half an hour. And I had seen Dan, all told, perhaps fifteen minutes!

At Orange we found everything in confusion, and everybody who could get out leaving the town. The story went that the Yankee cavalry under Stoneman would soon be in possession of it. We were glad enough to keep our seats and go straight through to Richmond, and it was well that we did, for behind us came Stoneman's cavalry close on our heels and tearing up bridges as they came. The railroad track at Trevillian's was torn up just after we passed over it. Richmond was in a state of great excitement. Couriers were passing to and fro between the army and the executive offices, stirring news kept pouring in, and the newspapers were in a fever. Tidings from the first battle of the Wilderness began coming in. Lee's army and "Fighting Joe" Hooker's were grappling with each other there like tigers in a jungle. Stuart, our great cavalry leader, had caught up Jackson's mantle as it fell, and was riding around in that valley of death, charging his men to "Remember Jackson!" and singing in that cheery voice of his which only death could drown: "Old Joe Hooker, won't you Come Out of the Wilderness?" Then came news of victory and Richmond was wild with joy and wild with woe as well. In many homes were vacant chairs because of that battle in the Wilderness, and from Petersburg, twenty miles away, came the sound of mourning, Rachel weeping for her children and refusing to be comforted because they were not.

It was from Petersburg that I was summoned to Culpeper by Dan, who felt that the army might have a long enough breathing spell there for me to pay him at least a visit. When I got to Mr. Bradford's, where he had engaged board for me, I found General Stuart's headquarters in the yard. He and his staff were boarders at Mr. Bradford's, and I ate at the same table with the flower of the Southern cavalry. Unfortunately for me, Dan's command was stationed at a distance of several miles, and I could not see as much of him as I had hoped. He met me the day of my arrival, rode by once or twice, took one or two meals with me, and then it seemed that for all I saw of him I might as well have remained in Petersburg.

My seat at table was next to that of General Stuart, and for vis-à-vis I had Colonel John Esten Cooke. Colonel Cooke was a glum old thing, but General Stuart was so delightful that he compensated for everything. In a short time I was completely at my ease with him, and long before he left I had grown to love and trust him.

Chapter XIX

My Comrade General Jeb Stuart

ONE day General Stuart asked me in a teasing way:

"You wouldn't really like to see Dan Grey, would you?"

"Oh, but I would, general," I said, in too dead earnest to give raillery for raillery.

"I don't believe you really want to see Dan Grey."

"Well, I don't, then," a bit sullenly.

"What a pity! You might see him now, if you really wanted to."

I wouldn't notice such a frivolous remark.

Dinner over, we went out on the veranda, as usual, and General Stuart dropped into a chair beside me.

"I really thought you rather liked Dan Grey, but it seems I was mistaken. And you really don't want to see him? Sad - I must tell him and condole with him."

I tried to bury myself in a book I was reading and pay no attention to him. A miserable old book it was - Children of the Abbey, or something like it - that I had picked up somewhere at Mr. Bradford's. Hereafter, if I write "Aunt Sally's" instead of Mr. Bradford's, please understand that one and the same place is meant. Aunt Sally was Mr. Bradford's wife, and I reckon the first term best describes the place.

"You wouldn't really rather have Dan Grey sitting here in this chair beside you than me?" continued my tease.

I lifted my eyes to him wet with vexation and longing.

"I'll make you smile now!" he said. "Do you want to see Dan?"

"Yes, I do. I want to see him dreadfully, but I am not going to tell you so again."

"You will if I command you to, won't you? If you are in the cavalry I am your superior officer, you know. I can even make Dan mind what I say, can't I? If you are refractory, I can command Dan to bring you to terms."

"I'd like to see Dan do it! You may be Commander-in-chief of the cavalry, but you aren't commander-in-chief of me - you or Dan either."

"It seems not," he commented meekly. "You are the most insubordinate little rebel I ever saw. I have a great mind to court-martial you - no, I believe I'll send for Dan and let him do it."

He called a courier, and wrote a despatch in regular form, ordering Major Dan Grey to report at once to General Stuart. Then he added a little private note to Dan which had for a postscript:

"Sweet Nellie is by my side."

"That will bring him in a hurry!" laughed Stuart.

The courier, not knowing but that the fate of the Confederacy depended upon that despatch, put spurs to his horse, galloped down the road and out of sight. I suppose he ran his horse all the way, and that Dan ran his all the way back, for before General Stuart left the veranda Dan galloped into the yard.

"I'll get the first kiss!" said General Stuart, still teasingly.

He leaped from the porch and ran across the yard, I tearing after him. I caught up and passed him, and looking back at him from Dan's arms, into which I had stumbled, breathless and panting, I laughed out: "I can beat the Yankees getting out of your way!"

Perhaps this race and General Stuart's love of teasing may seem undignified conduct for the chief of the Southern cavalry, but it is history and it is fun, and those who knew him did not fail in respect to Stuart. Many of us loved the ground he walked on. His boyish spirits and his genial, sunny temperament helped to make him the idol of the cavalry and the inspiration of his soldiers, and kept heart in them no matter what happened.

That was a lovely evening. General Stuart had Sweeny, his banjo-player, in. Sweeny was a dignified, solemn-looking man, but couldn't he play merry tunes on that banjo, and sad ones too! making you laugh and cry with his playing and his singing.

"When the sad, chilly winds of December Stole my flowers, my companions, from me."

That was one of his mournful favorites. And you heard the jingle of spurs in his rollicking:

"If you want a good time, Jine the cavalry, Bully boys, hey!"

We called for "Old Joe Hooker, won't you Come Out of the Wilderness?" and "O Johnny Booker, help this Nigger!" and "O Lord, Ladies, don't you mind Stephen!" and "Sweet Evelina," and - oh! I can't remember them all, but if you choose to read Esten Cooke, he will tell you all about Sweeny's songs and banjo. Stuart sang "The Dew is on the Blossom" and "The Bugles sang Truce." He made Sweeny give, twice over, "Sweet Nellie is by my Side," and sat himself down beside me, and tried to tease Dan because he sat at table with me every day and Dan couldn't. In spite of everything I was very happy in those old days at the Bradfords'! I was not yet out of my teens, you know; so I hope I was not very much to blame because I was always ready for a romp across that lawn at Mr. Bradford's with the commander-in-chief of the Southern cavalry. His was the gentlest, merriest, sweetest-tempered soul I ever knew. He was always ready to sympathize with me, to tease me, and to help me. Whenever he teased me out of conceit with myself or him, he always would put me in a good humor by saying nice things about Dan, or sending a courier after him.

He had an idea that I was very plucky, and in after days when I was ready to show the white feather, Dan would shame me by asking, "What would General Stuart say?"

Mr. Bradford and his wife, "Aunt Sally," were characters. Mr. Bradford was a very quiet, peaceable man; Aunt Sally was strong-minded, and had a tongue and mind of her own. Mr. Bradford had a good deal of property and stayed out of the army to take care of it. I think Aunt Sally made him stay out of the war for this reason, but she made home about as hot for him as the field would have been. I can't think he stayed at home to keep out of war, for he was in war all the time. Aunt Sally continually twitted him with staying at home, although she made him do it. She was always sure to do this when the table was filled with Confederate officers.

"The place for a man," she would say, "is on the field. Just give me the chance to fight! Just give me the chance to fight, and see where I'll be!"

And General Stuart would convulse me by whispering: "I don't think she needs a chance to fight, do you?"

Sometimes when Aunt Sally's harangue would begin the general would whisper, "Aunt Sally's getting herself in battle array," or "The batteries have limbered up," or "Aunt Sally's scaled the breastworks," and Mr. Bradford's meek and inoffensive face would make the situation funnier. He would mildly help the boarders to the dish in front of him and endeavor feebly to turn the conversation into a peaceful and safe direction, though this never had the slightest effect upon his belligerent wife.

One day - it was about the time of Stuart's historical grand review - Mr. Bradford invited all the cavalry generals whose forces were stationed around us to dine with the commander- in-chief of the cavalry. He would never have dared to do this if Aunt Sally had been at home, but Aunt Sally at this auspicious moment was in Washington, where we all hoped the fortunes of war and shopping would keep her indefinitely. Her niece, Miss Morse, and I sat down, the only ladies present, at a table with eighteen Confederate generals. Miss Molly and I were at first a trifle embarrassed at being the only ladies, but they were all refined and well-bred, and soon put us at our ease. General Wade Hampton led me in to dinner, and I sat between him and General Ramseur. General Ramseur was young and exceedingly handsome, and a paralyzed arm which was folded across his breast made him all the more attractive.

"If you sit next me, Mrs. Grey," he said with a little embarrassment, "you will have to cut up my dinner for me. I am afraid that will be putting you to a great deal of trouble. Perhaps I had better change my seat."

"Oh, no!" I said, "I will be very glad - if I can be satisfactory."

He smiled. "Thank you. I am always both glad and sorry to impose upon a lady this service. I am sorry, you know, to tax a lady with it, but then, she always does it better than a man."

I had been studying his face, and now, for want of something more sensible I said:

"If I am to feed you, General Ramseur, I must measure your mouth."

It happened that there was dead silence at the table when this silly speech of mine was made. Everybody was listening.

"Madam," said the handsome general, blushing and smiling, "I am entirely willing that you should."

I caught a mischievous light in General Stuart's merry eyes, and blushed furiously. Then I followed his laugh, and the whole table roared.

"I will tell Dan Grey!" cried Stuart.

"I will tell Dan Grey!" ran around the table like a chorus.

But I fed my handsome general all the same.

It was while I was at Mr. Bradford's that one of the most stirring events in Confederate history occurred. This was the trampling down of John Minor Botts's corn. Very good corn it was, dropped and hilled by Southern negroes and growing on a large, fine plantation next to Mr. Bradford's; and a very nice gentleman Mr. Botts was, too; but a field of corn, however good, and a private citizen, however estimable, are scarcely matters of national or international importance. The trouble was that John Minor Botts was on the Northern side and the corn was on the Southern side, and that Stuart held a grand review on the Southern side and the corn got trampled down. The fame of that corn went abroad into all the land. Northern and Southern papers vied with each other in editorials and special articles, families who had been friends for generations stopped speaking and do not speak to this day because of it, more than one hard blow was exchanged for and against it, and it brought down vituperation upon Stuart's head. And yet I was present at that naughty grand review - which left sorrowful memory on many hearts because of the battle following fast upon it - and I can testify that General Stuart went there to review the troops, not to trample down the corn.

Afterward John Minor Botts came over to see General Stuart and to quarrel about that corn. All that I can remember of how the general took Mr. Botts's visit and effort to quarrel was that Stuart wouldn't quarrel - whatever it was he said to Mr. Botts he got to laughing when he said it. Our colored Abigail told us with bated breath that "Mr. Botts ripped and rarred and snorted, but Genrul Stuart warn't put out none at all."

There had been many reviews that week, all of them merely by way of preparation and practice for that famous grand review before the battle of Brandy or Fleetwood, but it is only of this particular grand review I have many lively memories. Aunt Sally was away, and we attended it in state. Mr. Bradford had out the ancient and honorable family carriage and two shadowy horses, relics of days when corn was in plenty and wheat not merely a dream of the past, and we went in it to the review along with many other carriages and horses, whose title to respect lay, alas! solely in the past.

That was a day to remember! Lee's whole army was in Culpeper. Pennsylvania and Gettysburg were before it, and the army was making ready for invasion. On a knoll where a Confederate flag was planted and surrounded by his staff sat General Lee on horseback; before him, with a rebel yell, dashed Stuart and his eight thousand cavalry. There was a sham battle. Charging and countercharging went on, rebels yelled and artillery thundered. Every time the cannons were fired we would pile out of our carriage, and as soon as the cannonading ceased we would pile back again. General Stuart happened to ride up once just as we were getting out.

"Why don't you ladies sit still and enjoy the fun?" he asked in amazement.

"We are afraid the horses might take fright and run away," we answered.

I shall never forget his ringing laugh. Our lean and spiritless steeds had too little life in them to run for anything - they hardly pricked up their ears when the guns went off.

How well I remember Stuart as he looked that day! He wore a fine new uniform, brilliant with gold lace, buff gauntlets reaching to his elbows, and a canary-colored silk sash with tasseled ends. His hat, a soft, broad brimmed felt, was caught up at the side with a gold star and carried a sweeping plume; his high, patent-leather cavalry boots were trimmed with gold. He wore spurs of solid gold, the gift of some Maryland ladies - he was very proud of those spurs - and his horse was coal black and glossy as silk. And how happy he was - how full of faith in the Confederacy and himself!

My own cavalry officer was there, resplendent in his new uniform - I had had it made up for him in Richmond. Dan was very proud of the way I got that uniform. He was almost ready to credit himself with having put me up to running the blockade! He told General Stuart its history, and that is how a greatness not always easy to sustain had been thrust upon me. General Stuart thought me very brave - or said he thought so. The maneuvers of Dan's command were on such a distant part of the field that I could not see him well with the naked eye, and General Stuart lent me his field-glasses The next morning, just as gray dawn was breaking, some one called under my window, and gravel rattled against the pane. I got up and looked out sleepily. My first thought was that it might be Dan. There was not enough light for me to see very well what was happening on the lawn, but I could make out that the cavalry were mounted and moving, and under my window I saw a figure on horseback.

"Is that Mrs. Grey?"

"Yes. What is the matter?"

"General Stuart sent me for his field-glasses. I am sorry to disturb you, but it couldn't be helped."

I tied a string around the glasses and lowered them.

"What's the matter? Where is the cavalry going?"

"To Brandy Station. Reckon we'll have some hot fighting soon," and the orderly wheeled and rode away.

I stayed up and dressed, and thought of Dan, and wished I could know if he was to be in the coming engagement, and that I could see him first. But I didn't see him all day.

Chapter XX

“Whose Business Tis To Die”

IN forty-eight hours we knew that the surmise of the orderly was correct - there was enough fighting. The first cannon-ball which tore through the air at Brandy was only too grave assurance of the fact. All day men were hurrying past the house, deserters from both armies getting away from the scene of bloodshed and thunder as quickly as possible. Then came the procession of the dead and wounded, some in ambulances, some in carts, some on the shoulders of friends.

In the afternoon we began to hear rumors giving names of the killed and wounded. I listened with my heart in my throat for Dan’s name, but I did not hear it. I heard no news whatever of him all day - all day I could only hope that no news was good news, and all day that ghastly procession dragged heavily by. Among names of the killed I heard that of Colonel Sol Williams. A day or two before the battle of Brandy he had returned from a furlough to Petersburg, where he had gone to marry a lovely woman, a friend of mine. The day before he was killed he had sat at table with me, chatting pleasantly of mutual friends at home from whom he had brought messages, brimful of happiness, and of the charming wife he had won! As the day waned I sat in my room, wretched and miserable, thinking of my friend who was at once a bride and a widow, and fearing for myself, whose husband even at that moment might be falling under his death wound. I was aroused by hearing the voices of men, subdued but excited, on the stairway leading to my room. I ran out and saw several men of rank and Mr. Bradford on the stairway talking excitedly, and I heard my name spoken.

"What's the matter, gentlemen?" I asked with forced calmness.

They looked up at me in a stupid, masculine sort of way, as if they had something disagreeable to say and didn't want to say it. I could shake those men now, when I think of how stupid they were! They were listening to Mr. Bradford, and I don't think they really caught my question, nor did my manner betray to them how fast my heart was beating, but they were stupid, nevertheless. I could hardly get the next words out:

"Is Dan hurt?"

This time my voice was so low that they did not hear it at all.

"For God's sake, gentlemen," I cried out, "tell me if my husband is wounded or dead."

"Neither, madam!" several voices answered instantly, and the officer nearest me, thinking I was going to fall, sprang quickly to my side. I gathered myself together, and they told me their business, and I saw why my presence had embarrassed them - they wanted my room for the wounded. A funny thing had happened, incongruous as it was, in their telling me that my fears for Dan were groundless. When I asked, "Is Dan hurt?" one of them had answered, "No, ma'am; it's General Rooney Lee;" and I had said, "Thank God!" I can't describe the look of horror with which they heard me.

"These gentlemen," began Mr. Bradford, who was always afraid to speak his mind, "wanted to bring General Lee here, and I didn't have a place to put him, and I was telling 'em that I thought that - maybe - you would give him your room. I could fix up a lounge for you somewhere."

"Of course I will! I shall be delighted to give up my room, or do anything else I can for General Lee."

I busied myself getting my room ready for General "Rooney," but he was not brought to Mr. Bradford's, after all;

his men were afraid that he might be captured too easily at Mr. Bradford's. As night came on the yard filled up with soldiers. In the lawn, the road, the backyard, the porches, the outhouses, everywhere, there were soldiers. You could not set your foot down without putting it on a soldier; if you thrust your hand out of a window you touched a soldier's back or shoulder, his carbine or his musket. The place was crowded not only with cavalry, but with infantry and artillery, and still they kept on coming. I had not heard from Dan. It was late supper-time. I had no heart for supper, and I felt almost too shaken to present myself at the table, but as I passed the dining-room in my restless rovings I saw General Stuart's back, and went in and sat by him.

"General," I said, "can you tell me anything of Dan?"

"He is neither killed nor wounded. I know that much. Is not that enough?"

"Yes, thank God!

"Oh, general! I wish this war was over!" I said again.

"I, too, my child!" He spoke with more than Stuart's sadness and gravity, then, remembering himself, he added quickly in his own cheery fashion, "But we've got to whip these Yankees first!"

He finished his cup of coffee (the kind in Common use, made of corn which had been roasted, parched, and ground), and then went on telling me about Dan.

"He has borne himself gallantly, as he always does, and as you know without my telling you. I don't know where he is, but he will be along presently."

And at that moment Dan walked in, without a coat, and with the rest of that new uniform a perfect fright. He was covered with dust and ashes and gunpowder, and he looked haggard and jaded. He sat down between General Stuart and me, too tired to talk; but after eating some supper, he felt better, and began discussing the battle and relating some incidents. He took a card out of his pocket and handed it to General Stuart.

"A Federal officer who is about done for, poor fellow, handed me that just now. I don't know the name. He couldn't talk."

"I do!" General Stuart exclaimed, with quick, strong interest. "Where did you see him? This is the name of one of my classmates at West Point."

"I saw him on the roadside as I came on to supper. While riding along I heard a strange sound, something like a groan, yet different from any groan I ever heard - the strangest, most uncanny sound imaginable. I dismounted and began to look around for it, and I found a Yankee soldier lying in a ditch by the roadside. I couldn't see that any legs or arms were broken, nor that he was wounded at all. I felt him all over, and asked what was the matter. He didn't speak, and I saw that he had been trying to direct my attention to his face. He tried very hard to speak, but only succeeded in emitting the strange sound I had heard before; and on examining his face closely, and moving the whiskers aside, I found that he was shot through both jaws. He made the same noise again, put his hand in his pocket, and gave me this card, with another pitiful effort to speak. I put my coat under his head, laid some brush across the ditch to hide him, and promised to go back for him in an ambulance."

"Thank you, in my own behalf!" General Stuart said warmly.

"Perhaps, poor fellow," said Dan, "he took chances on that card's reaching you. Seeing my uniform of major of cavalry, he may not have considered it impossible that you should hear of his condition through me."

"When you have finished your supper, major, we will go after him."

Tired as they both were, they went out and attended personally to the relief of the poor fellow by the roadside. General Stuart had everything done for him that was possible, smoothed his last moments, and grieved over him as deeply as if his classmate had not been his enemy.

Another sad thing among the sorrows of that supper was when Colonel Sol Williams's brother-in-law, John Pegram, came in, and sat down in our midst. General Stuart went up to him, and wrung his hand in a silence that even the dauntless Stuart's lips were too tremulous at once to break. When he could speak he said:

"I grieve for myself as for you, lieutenant, but it was a death that any one of us might be proud to die."

Even then the shadow and glory of his own death was not far from him.

Colonel Williams had been Lieutenant Pegram's superior officer as well as brother-in-law. It had been his sorrowful lot to take the body of his colonel on his horse in front of him, and carry it to a house where it could be reverently cared for until he could send it home to bride and kindred. He had cut a lock of hair from the dead, and when the troops went off to Pennsylvania, he gave it to me for his sister. I shall never forget that supper hour, or how the unhappy young fellow looked when he came in among us after his ride with the dead, and I shall never forget how I felt about that poor young Federal soldier who was wounded in the jaws and couldn't speak, and how I felt about the women who loved him far away; I began to feel that war was an utterly unjustifiable thing, and that the virtues of valor, loyalty, devotion which it brings out had better be brought out some other way. If General Rooney Lee didn't take my room, I gave it up all the same. Two wounded men were put into it. There were a number of wounded men in the house, and, of course, everybody gave way to their comfort. All but my two were removed in a day or two, but here these two were, and here they were when Aunt Sally came home. Her home coming was after a fashion that turned our mourning into righteous and wholesome wrath. We were sitting on the porch one afternoon, free and easy in our minds and believing Aunt Sally away in distant Washington, when we noted a small object far off down the road. As it crawled nearer and nearer we perceived that it was an ox-cart; we saw the driver, and behind him somebody else sitting on a trunk.

"Good gracious! that's Aunt Sally!" cried Mr. Bradford in consternation.

We were all dreadfully sorry, but it couldn't be helped.

She climbed off the cart at the gate, and called for some negro to come get her trunk. Mr. Bradford had already found one, and was running to the rescue. In fact he had been running in a half dozen different directions ever since he had spied Aunt Sally. He looked as if his wits had left him and as if he were racing around in a circle.

"You orter been on hand to he'p me off 'o that kyart," she told him. "It do look like when a man's wife's been away this long time he might be on hand to he'p her off the kyart."

As she came up the walk she said the yard looked awful torn and "trompled down"; that she was afraid she would find it so soon as she heard that the place had been camping ground for the whole army and her away and nobody there to manage the army as she could have done. She greeted me and her niece, and in the same breath told her niece that there was some mud on the steps which ought to be washed off. Then she went into the house, taking off her things and remarking on "things that ought to be done." Presently there was a great stir in the house; she had found out the wounded men. She commented on their presence in such a loud voice that we heard it on the porch, and the men themselves must have heard it.

"Just like Mr. Bradford! If I had been here it wouldn't have happened. The idea! Turning the house into a hospital! I won't have it! Nobody knows who they are. I can't have 'em on my best beds, and between my best sheets and blankets. Dirty, common soldiers! I never heard of such a thing!"

And she got them out before supper.

There was an office in the yard and she had them taken to this. They had to be carried past us, and I can see them now, poor, mortified, shame-faced fellows! I was as afraid of Aunt

Sally as of a rattlesnake, but I think I could have shaken her then!

Little it was that I saw of Dan or any of my army friends after the battle of Brandy. The cavalry was too busy watching Hooker's, while our infantry was pushing on toward Pennsylvania, to spare any time to lighter matters. Every day the boys in gray marched by on their way North.

I watched from the porch and windows if by any means I might catch sight of Dan. But his way did not lie by Bradford's. One morning, however, I saw General Stuart riding by at the head of a large command. I thought they were going to stop and camp at Mr. Bradford's, perhaps, but I was mistaken. As soon as I saw that they were going by without stopping, I ran to the fence and beckoned to General Stuart. He had seen me on the porch, and rode up to the fence at once.

"Aren't you going to stop at all?" I asked.

"Not to-day. In fact we're off for some time now."

"Is Dan going?"

"Yes. He's ahead now with General Chambliss."

"Am I not to see him at all, General Stuart?" I said, trying hard to keep my lip from quivering - I had a reputation to keep up with him.

But he saw the quiver.

"You can go on with the army if you want to," he said in quick sympathy. "I will give you an ambulance. You can carry your own maid along, have your own tent, and have your husband with you. I will do anything I can for your comfort. You would nurse our poor fellows when they get hurt, and be no end of good to us. But it would be awfully hard on you."

"I wouldn't mind the hardships," I answered, "but you know Dan won't let me go. I have begged him several times to let me live in camp with him. I could nurse the sick and wounded, and take care of him if he was shot, and I wouldn't be a bit of trouble; and I could patch for the soldiers. Oh, I'd love to do it! If you come up with him, General Stuart, ask him to let me go, and if he says yes, send the ambulance."

"I'll promise him what I promised you," he said, smiling kindly. "Good-by now. I'll ride on and send him back to say good-by to you, if I can manage it. Then you can talk him into letting you come with us."

I climbed up on the fence to shake hands with him and to say good-by, and I had another word for him. Beneath my dress and next my skin was a little Catholic medal which had been blessed by my confessor. It hung around my neck by a slender chain. I unclasped the chain, drew forth the medal and gave it to him, my eyes brimming with tears.

"It has been blessed by Father Mulvey," I said. "Wear it about your neck. Maybe it will bring you back safe."

I was leaning upon the horse's neck, crying as if my heart would break. General Stuart's own eyes were dim.

"Good-by," I said, "and if you can send Dan back I thank you for us both - I thank you anyway for thinking of it; but - the South and his duty first. Good-by, and Go bless you, General Stuart!"

That was the last time I ever saw him, the last time that knightly hand clasped mine. Before he rode away he said some cheerful, hopeful words, and looked back at me with the glint of merry mischief in his eyes, threatening to tell Dan Grey that I was losing my good repute for bravery. Dan did not come back to say good-by. I had a little note which he contrived to send me in some way. It was only a hasty scrawl, full of good-bys and God bless yous.

After saying good-by to General Stuart I returned to the house. Esten Cooke sat at a table writing. He was preparing some official papers for General Stuart, I think, and had been left behind for that purpose. I understood him to answer one of my question to the effect that he was going to follow the cavalry presently.

"Colonel Cooke," I asked humbly enough, for I was ready then to take information and advice from anybody, "how long do you think it will be before the army comes back?"

"Can't say, madam."

"Would you advise me to wait here until is return?"

"Can't say, madam."

"Would you advise me to go to Richmond?"

"Madam, I would advise you to go to Richmond."

"You think then it will be some time before the army returns?"

"I can't say, madam?"

I felt like shaking him and asking: "What can you say?" He may have been a brave soldier and written nice books and all that, but I think John Esten Cooke was a very dull, disagreeable man.

I waited several days, but as I got nothing further from Dan than the little note - which was bare of advice because, perhaps, he didn't have time to write more, and because he may not have known how to advise me - I took John Esten Cooke's advice and went to Richmond. I stopped there only a very short time, and then went on to Petersburg, where mother was. Reunion with her was compensation for many troubles, and then, too, she needed me. She had not heard from Milicent since my departure for Culpeper. Then a letter had reached us through the agency of Mr. Cridland, in which Milicent had stated her purpose of coming to us as soon as she could get a pass - a thing it was every day becoming more difficult to secure - for she was determined upon reaching us before the cold weather came again. Since that letter there had been absolute silence.

Then came upon us that awful July of , and the battle of Gettysburg, the beginning of the end. Virginians fell by hundreds in that fight, and Pickett's charge goes down to history along with Balaklava and Thermopylae. There were more vacant chairs in Virginia, already desolate - there were more broken hearts for which Heaven alone held balm. "When Italy's made, for what good is it done if we have not a son?" Again the angel of death had passed me by. But my heart bled for my friends who were dead on that red field far away - for my friends who mourned and could not be comforted.

One of our wounded, whose father brought him home to be nursed, bore to me a letter from my husband and a package from General Stuart. The package contained a photograph of himself that he had promised me, and a note, bright, genial, merry, like himself. That picture is hanging on my wall now. On the back is written by a hand long crumbled into dust, "To her who in being a devoted wife did not forget to be a true patriot." The eyes smile down upon us as I lift my little granddaughter up to kiss my gallant cavalier's lips, and as she lisps his name my heart leaps to the memory of his dauntless life and death.

He was shot one beautiful May morning in while trying to prevent Sheridan's approach to Richmond. It was at Yellow Tavern - a dismantled old tavern not many miles from the Confederate capital - that he fell, and Colonel Venable, who was serving with him at the time and near him when he fell, helped, if I remember aright, to shroud him. When he told me what he could of General Stuart's last hours, he said:

"There was a little Catholic medal around his neck, Nell. Did you give him that? We left it on him."

And so passes from this poor history my beloved and loyal friend, my cavalry hero and good comrade. Virginia holds his dust sacred, and in history he sits at the Round Table of all true-souled and gentle knights.

Chapter XXI

Rescued By The Foe

Milicent's arrest in Washington as related by herself.

I PASSED May and a part of the summer of in fruitless efforts to get a pass to Virginia. This was when the Civil War was at its whitest heat, and I was in the city of Baltimore, where a word was construed into treason, and messages and letters were contrived to and from the South only by means of strategy. One by one my plans failed. Then came the battle of Gettysburg, and as I heard of our reverses I felt an almost helpless lethargy stealing over me - as if I should ever see Nell or mother again. How long the war would last, and what would be the end of it none could tell. Nell and mother were in a besieged country, and the blockade between us seemed an impassable wall. The long silence was becoming unbearable as I slowly realized that it might become the silence of death and I not know.

At last came news which I thought affected them, and which startled me into instant energy.

One morning my friend, Miss Barnett, a beautiful girl, rushed into my room, and, throwing herself on the floor beside me, began telling me with sobs and tears that my brother-in-law, Major Grey, or his brother Dick, was a prisoner in the Old Capitol at Washington. She begged me to go at once and see what I could do. If I could not find some way of helping the prisoner to freedom, I could at least add to his comfort in prison.

"You could at least show him that he was remembered,"

she said. "You could take some little delicacies which would be grateful to a prisoner. I will help you to get them up."

Poor Isabelle! It was one of the tragedies of the war. She was too wretched to attempt any concealment.

"You see, if I had any right to go myself I would not ask you to go for me. If I were even engaged to him - but I am not. You see, it couldn't be. But, O Millie! I wish there wasn't any war that I might be my love's betrothed and go to him!"

For a minute her proposition daunted me. To rush into Washington, a Southern woman, alone and unprotected; to be surrounded on all sides by the Government officials and spies whose business it was to watch and report every careless word and act of any one who was known to be interested in the South or in Southerners - the undertaking seemed desperate. But there were Isabelle's tearful eyes, and there was the fear that Nell's husband might be the prisoner. I determined to make the trip at all hazards.

Together we made purchases of what we considered the most tempting delicacies to take to an invalid or prisoner. There were cheeses, crackers, oranges, lemons, jellies; and we did not forget to add to our stock wine, whisky, pipes, and tobacco. Isabelle herself sent a box of fine cigars, a costly gift, for the war with the Southern States affected the price of tobacco.

The next morning I started off by myself to Washington in fear and trembling. Taking a hack there, and trusting to a kind Providence for guidance and protection drove first to the office of the provost marshal for a permit. On entering his office, to my consternation I recognized in him the judge-advocate under whose protection, our truce boat had gone to Richmond not many months before with the distinct understanding that her passengers were not to return from Dixie while the war lasted. But it was too late to retreat. Rallying all my courage and self-control I greeted him as a stranger, asking whether or not I was addressing Judge Turner. Answered in the affirmative, I requested permission to visit the prisoners in the Old Capitol.

While I was talking he looked up and a glance almost of recognition lighted his face. It was succeeded by a more scrutinizing regard as I stood in perfectly assumed unconsciousness before him. Bowing, he asked me to be seated, and to repeat my petition. Others were waiting their turn, and his answer was prompt:

"Certainly, madam. You can see two prisoners mentioned, or any one you wish, and take with you what you please."

An easy job certainly!

My heart grew light; I arose to go, thanking the judge cordially.

He said: "One moment, madam."

I went back, and he handed me a pen, ink, and slip of paper, saying:

"Just sign this, please. It is of no consequence at all - a mere matter of form - only you can not see your friends without it."

There spread out before me was the ironclad oath!

Without a moment's hesitation I replied:

"The oath, Judge Turner! Am I to sign that? I can not! and never will!"

He smiled apologetically and said:

"It is of no consequence - only a little form that we have to insist on. Sign it, and you can go to your friends."

"If it is of no consequence to your side, provost, why should it be of so much to mine that I can not see my friends without it?"

He smiled, and still held the pen out to me.

"No! never!" I said. "Then I can not help you. I am sorry, You must apply at military headquarters."

He kindly directed me to the same. I hurried down the steps, jumped into my hack, and drove quickly to the War Department. Here I made my request again and again met with the same polite consent backed with the oath. Again I refused and turned to go, when one of the officers kindly suggested:

"Make application to the officer at the Old Capitol. He may permit you to see the prisoners without oath, though I fear not."

As there was not much time left before my train would start for Baltimore, I urged my driver to do his best, and we sped on in haste until we stopped before the gloomy, formidable-looking prison of the Old Capitol. With the permission of the guard I entered. The officer in command received me with kindness and courtesy, and with his consent I was about to ascend the stairs when he extended his hand, saying:

"The oath, if you please. I presume you took it at the War Department, and have your pass."

Again I was foiled. This was my last chance. There was no use pleading, and I was in despair. I leaned on a chair to rest a moment before leaving the room, defeated. I had not a word to say, and I did not say a word. I suppose my deep dejection touched him. I was about to go when he said with great kindness:

"Wait here near these steps. I will send up an order, and if he is there, he can come to the railing and you can speak to him, and send him anything you wish. But you can not go up."

An orderly ascended with the message, and I waited at the steps, watching anxiously for Dan or Dick to appear at the railing. I did not have many minutes to wait. The orderly returned with the reply that Lieutenant - not Major - Grey had been exchanged that very morning, and was now on his way home. Happy for Nell and Isabelle and myself, I poured out my thanks to the officer in command for helping me to such good news, and asked his permission to send the large basket of good things I had brought to the other prisoners. He gave it, and I saw the orderly again mount the stairs, burdened this time with good wishes and my still more substantial and acceptable offering. As I went out, passing again through the prison gates, my driver whispered in the most excited manner:

"Lady! lady! do take care! The prisoners are all at the windows, and if you look up or speak to them we will both be arrested instantly."

I seated myself quickly, and then, in spite of all fears and warnings, glanced up, to see the windows filled with faces, and hands and handkerchiefs waving to me inside the bars. As we dashed forward, I leaned out of the window waving my handkerchief in vigorous response. In the excitement, the enthusiasm of the moment, I lost all sense of fear or danger - my whole heart was with those desolate, homesick Confederates behind the bars. Fortunately the driver was frightened out of his wits and drove like mad, or we should never have gotten to the train in time.

I had been fortunate enough to find in my driver a strong, if secret, sympathizer with the South. As I bade him good-by, and thanked him for the care and promptness with which he had carried me about, and for his unheeded warning as well, he said:

"Oh, lady, lady, you ran a great risk when you waved that handkerchief! I saw it and drove as fast as I could to get you away from there. It is a wonder we were not arrested."

I stepped on the car, and was taking my seat, when a hand lightly touched my shoulder from behind, and I heard myself arrested by a name that was not mine. Behind me stood a sergeant in the United States uniform, who informed me that I was his prisoner.

I tried to shrink away from him.

"That is not my name," I said.

Still he kept that light grip on my shoulder. I felt sick. The day had been a long one of exercise and excitement. I had eaten nothing since my early breakfast of a cracker and a cup of coffee, and I was physically weak. The terror of the situation, the full foolhardiness of my undertaking flashed upon me. Alone in Washington, not a friend near, and under arrest!

For an instant everything whirled around me, and I fell back against the breast of the sergeant; but as instantly I pulled myself together and stood erect.

"You are mistaken," I said quietly, "I am not the person you have mentioned."

And I threw back my heavy mourning veil and looked my captor full in the face.

"Ain't you? It's widow's weeds this time!"

These words were spoken sarcastically by a man in civilian dress who was with the sergeant - a detective, I suppose.

"I am Mrs. Milicent Duncan Norman, of Baltimore," I said firmly. "You can telegraph to No. - Charles Street and see. You will please remove your hand," I continued. "If necessary I will go with you, but I am not the person you wish to arrest. You are making a mistake."

I turned my face full to the light, and stood, calm and composed, though my knees were trembling under me, and I felt as if I should faint. I saw Bobby at home waiting for me!

"I must stay over if you insist," I repeated, "but I hope you will permit me to convince you of your mistake. It would be extremely inconvenient to me to be detained here. I left Baltimore this morning, and my little boy has been without me all day. He will cry himself sick if I don't get home tonight."

In spite of all I could do my lips quivered.

"I am sorry, madam," said my sergeant, more respectfully than he had hitherto spoken, "but you will have to come with me. If it is as you say, you can telegraph and satisfy the authorities very quickly."

My arrest had attracted some attention. I saw that people in the car were gathering around me, and I saw curiosity in some faces, sympathy in some, but among all those faces none that I knew. This was my first visit to Washington, and there was not a soul to identify me. There was nothing to do but to go and telegraph - if they would let me. I would have to miss my train. Bobby was watching from the window for me this very minute - Bobby would cry all night. I told the sergeant that I would go, and tried to follow him, and then everything grew dark around me, my head whirled, and I dropped across the seat nearest me.

I could not have been unconscious more than a second. The kind gentleman over whose seat I had fallen had caught me, and was slapping my face with a wet handkerchief, and assuring the sergeant that he knew by my face that I was perfectly harmless and ought not to be arrested, that he would bet anything on it, when a new passenger hurriedly entered the car and brushed squarely up against us.

The sergeant was saying: "We must hurry," and offering me his arm very courteously. "You will feel better when you get out in the air. And you will perhaps come out all right, and be able to go on to-morrow."

The newcomer looked over the sergeant's shoulder and saw me.

"Milicent!" he said, and clasped my hands.

It was a dear friend whom I had know in my girlhood days as Captain Warren.

"What is all this?" he asked quickly of the sergeant.

The sergeant was staggered, the little man in civilian's clothes cringed, the old man who had offered to bet on me was in the majority.

"We must get out of this, commodore," said the sergeant quickly, "the car is moving."

The commodore got out with us, lifted me bodily off the train, and then, as we stood together, while the sergeant explained, supported me with his arm. I was too weak and ill to hear their talk. I think I was very nearly in a faint while I stood, or tried to stand upright beside him.

He told me afterward that I had been arrested by mistake for some famous political spy in petticoats. He answered for me, made himself responsible in every way, lifted me into a carriage, and told the driver where to take us. I was too nearly dead to listen to what he said. As the carriage whirled along I tried to sit up, to lift my head, but every time I attempted it I grew blind and sick.

"I would not try to sit up just yet, Mrs. Norman," he said very kindly. "In a few minutes, perhaps, you can do so without risk, but I'd be very quiet now. In a little while I will hand you over to my wife - she is a wonderful nurse."

"My little boy is looking out of the window for me, waiting for me; he has been by himself all day," I sobbed.

"Ah! I am so sorry you have had this annoyance and detention. I wish I had boarded the car earlier; you should have gone on if I had. I was outside talking with some friends, and I did not jump on the train until she was about to move off, but I can telegraph to your friends, and you can go on tomorrow."

The ride in the open air had revived me, and I found now that I could sit up without fainting.

"You were going to Baltimore to-night," I said. "I am putting you to so much trouble."

"None at all. And if you were" - with a tremor in his voice - "I should be glad of it. Can you sit up? Ah! I am so glad you are better. When I first took you into this carriage I was afraid I would have to stop with you at the first doctor's office. We are nearly home now."

"You are very good," I said, still too weak not to speak with tears in my voice.

"I am fortunate - but too much at your expense, I am afraid. You forget how large my debt is. I shall never forget the old days in Norfolk and the kindness that was shown me by you and yours. I owe you a great deal, Mrs. Norman, as yourself and as your father's daughter. I shall never forget his charming hospitality. I am sorry you can't go on to Baltimore, but I am glad of my opportunity."

"That is a nice way to put it, commodore."

"A true way to put it, Mrs. Norman. Please don't be too sorry. Where is Nell? - Mrs. Grey, I suppose I should say. I can't think of the saucy little fairy who used to sit on my knee as a madam."

"I don't know just where Nell is, or how. The fortunes of war have separated me from her, and mother as well."

"And you are alone, without kindred, in Baltimore?"

"Yes, except my baby. I wish you could see Bobby - he is so sweet!"

"He must be."

"He has Nell's eyes and her golden curls - you remember?"

"Too well!"

"And her saucy sweet ways - wilful and almost bad - if he were not so sweet and true But I tire you. Mothers who talk about their babies bore people. I make many good resolves not to talk Bobby, and, break every one."

"You could never tire me. I am charmed to hear about your boy. Maybe you can find him a little sweetheart in my house. Here we are."

He lifted me out of the carriage and led me into the house.

"This is an old friend of mine, dear," he said to his wife. "She is sick and in trouble and I have brought her to you. Her father's home used to be my home in Norfolk. Mrs. Norman is Miss Duncan that was."

She had heard of me. He began to explain how he had met me, but she interrupted.

"I will come back and hear," she said, "when I have made Mrs. Norman comfortable. She looks worn-out. I must take her to her room and see what I can do to make her more at ease." While she was talking she had me in a chair, holding my hand, and giving me a glass of wine.

Commodore Warren took my Baltimore address, and went out saying he would send the telegrams at once - a special one to Bobby all by himself.

Then Mrs. Warren saw me to my room. As we passed through hallways and up the stairs, our feet sank into soft, thick carpets that gave back no sound. Through an open doorway I caught a glimpse of her own exquisite chamber and of a cozy nursery where children's gowns were laid out for the night. Everywhere around me were evidences of wealth, luxury, and refinement.

After a little rest I felt better.

As I went down to dinner I heard the street door open, and Commodore Warren's voice in the hall.

Then children's voices:

"Papa! papa!"

He was taking his children in his arms and kissing them, and I heard the glad murmur of his wife's welcome.

Together they took me in to their table, and showered upon me courtesies and loving kindness. Such a delightful dining-room it was - such lovely appointments and such perfect serving! and such charming hosts they made! The children are beautiful and well trained. They were brought into the parlor after dinner, and made great friends with me. You know children always like me, Nell. This trio took possession of me. They hovered around me, leaned against me, climbed into my lap, and the youngest went to sleep in my arms, her soft golden head nestled under my chin. We decided that she is to be Bobby's sweetheart. Their parents were afraid that I was not strong enough for such demonstrations, but I begged that they would not interrupt the little people, whose caresses really did me a world of good. But the commodore called the nurse when the baby dropped to sleep, and she took it to the nursery, the other children following her. By this time I was quite myself. A telegram had come from Isabelle, saying she was with Bobby and that Bobby was comforted.

Commodore and Mrs. Warren suggested that we should go to the opera. It was rather late to start, but the carriage would take us in a few minutes, and we should not miss more than the first act. A great singer was to be heard, and the commodore remembered that I was fond of music. When I objected on the score that I was not in opera dress and that my wardrobe was in Baltimore, they explained that they kept a private box, and that I could hear without being distinctly visible - if I was not too fatigued to think of going.

"Oh, no!" I said. "You know I love opera, and, thanks to you both, I am entirely rested and comfortable about Bobby."

Mrs. Warren ran up-stairs to dress while the carriage was being made ready. As for me, there was nothing to do but to put on my bonnet and cloak, so I sat still, and Commodore Warren drew up a chair in front of the sofa where I sat.

"This is like old times," he said.

I tried to keep them back, but somehow I felt the tears starting to my eyes.

He got up and walked to the other end of the room, and brought a book of drawings of queer places and people he had seen in his journeys around the world. While he was showing them to me he remarked:

"I've a box somewhere of curious toys picked up in various parts of the world at different times, and I think Master Bobby would be interested in them. We'll get Mrs. Warren to look it up, and I'll ask you to be kind enough to take it to him with my compliments. It may - in a measure - recompense him for his mother's absence to-night "

"Bobby will be delighted - if he is not robbing your children."

"My children," he laughed, "have a surfeit of toys from the four corners of the earth. They have almost lost appreciation of such hinge. By the way, has Nell" - he caught himself with a laugh - "Mrs. Grey, I should say, any little ones of her own?"

"Bobby is the only baby in the family; but he is enough to go around."

"I remember with profound gratitude the many expressions I used to receive of Nell's regard in those old days, and seeing on brings them back. Oh, forgive me - I know there have been many changes."

"Don't apologize," I said, smiling; "I am always glad to have old days and old friends recalled. Usually it does not shake me even to talk about father - it's a pleasure to think people remember him. In the first part of this evening I had not quite recovered from my arrest. But Richard is himself again now. I haven't forgotten how to be happy, and I'm going to enjoy this opera." And I did enjoy it.

Mrs. Warren took me to my train in her carriage; and there he met us to say good-by to me, and to tell me that he would see that I had a pass to Norfolk in a day or two. They both saw me comfortably seated, and after farewells were said and he had seen his wife to her carriage he stepped back on the cars with a handful of flowers for me.

"Is there nothing," he asked, "nothing that I can do for you? If you are ever in any trouble when I can help you, won't you let me know?"

I bowed my head.

"And Bobby - if there is ever anything I can do for your child, you will let me know?

"Good-by," he said, "it is good to meet old friends and find that neither time nor war changes them. Good-by - we shall see you again some day."

Isabelle was very happy when I told her that Dick was safe, and now that it was over she regretted having sent me into such dangers and tribulations.

"I ought to have gone," she said. "I could have taken the oath, you see, if they had asked me. And then, well, papa is known there, but - I couldn't ask papa to help Dick. He wouldn't have done anything for him."

Chapter XXII

WITH DAN AT CHARLOTTESVILLE

MILICENT always came as a soul comes.

The day after we got the batch of letters the door opened softly, and there she stood, holding Bobby by the hand. She had come so quietly that we did not know it until she stood in our midst. But Bobby was a veritable piece of flesh and blood. As soon as he saw it was grandma and auntie, he made a bound for us, and overwhelmed us with his noisy and affectionate greetings, while his mother submitted to being loved and kissed, and in her quiet way loved and kissed back again. Then she told us how she had come from Norfolk to Petersburg. It was a long, dreary trip.

"I went on a flag-of-truce train to Suffolk. Dr. Wright's family were on the train, and I spent the night with them. Bobby burned his throat at supper by swallowing tea too hot for him, and he did not rest well in the early part of the night and slept late the next day, and I was very anxious about him. This, and the difficulty in getting a conveyance, kept me at Dr. Wright's until the afternoon. By that time I had secured a mule-cart to take me to Ivor Station, on the Norfolk and Petersburg Railroad. Ivor, you know, is not more than twenty-five miles from Suffolk by the direct route, but the route we had to take for safety, as far as the Yankees and mud were concerned, was longer, and our one mule went slowly.

"The first afternoon we traveled till late in the night. Bobby would insist on driving the mule, and the driver humored him. In spite of the pain in his throat, he stood up against my knee and held the lines until, poor little tired fellow! he went to sleep holding thcm. I drew him on to my lap, covered him up, and we went on, the old negro, old mule, and baby all asleep. At last we stopped at a farmhouse to feed the mule. The woman who lived there asked me in. I laid Bobby down on her bed, dropped across it, and in five minutes was asleep myself. I don't know how many other people slept in that bed that night, but I know that the old woman, Bobby, and I slept in it. When I woke up it was several hours after daylight. Our breakfast the next morning was a typical Confederate, breakfast. My hostess gave me a drink made of parched wheat and corn which had been ground, a glass of milk, and some corn bread and bacon, and I enjoyed the meal and paid her cheerfully.

"We reached Ivor late that afternoon, my driver got his fee and departed, and Bobby and I were left to wait for the train. But we were not the only persons at the station; two other women were waiting at Ivor. If those two women could have had their way there would never have been another sunset on this earth. Their two sons were to be shot at sundown - they were watching for the sun to go down. Up and down, up and down, they walked in front of a tent where their sons under military guard awaited execution, and as they walked their eyes, swift and haggard, shifted from tent to sky and back again from sky to tent. As my train moved out of the station I glanced back. They were walking with feverish haste, and the sun hung low in the heavens."

"Hush, hush!" I cried, "I can't stand another word - I shall dream of those women all night. Tell me how you got here at last!"

"When I reached Pocahontas I meant to go to Jarrett's, and stop until I could find out where you were, but while I was looking around for a carriage who should I come upon but John, our old hackman. He told me that you were both out here at Uncle William's, and I made him drive me out."

Soon after my sister's arrival we moved into town and

boarded at Miss Anne Walker's, an old historic house then facing Washington Street, which runs east and west, paralleling the railroad at Jarrett's Hotel - or rather where Jarrett's used to stand - an ugly old hotel in the heart of the town. It was beside this railroad that I ran bareheaded along Washington Street some months later to get out of the way of the Yankee cannon. I was at Miss Anne's when Dan gave me leave to visit him at Charlottesville. His headquarters was a small cottage in sight of the university and of my window. He came to me every night - home was a student's room in the university - and very often I went with him in the morning to his cottage.

One morning as I sat in the cottage, turning a pair of Dan's old trousers, the door opened, and a fine-looking cavalry officer entered. Surprised to find a lady in occupation, he lifted his hat and started to withdraw. Then he hesitated, regarding me in a confused, doubtful fashion. Whereupon I in my turn began to stare at him.

"Isn't this John - John Mason?" I asked suddenly.

"That is my name," with a sweeping bow. "And are you not my old friend, Miss Nellie Duncan, of Norfolk?"

"Yes," I answered smiling, "but you know I have a third name now."

"Of course. Unpleasant facts are always hard to remember. I heard of your marriage, certainly, but for the moment the remembrance of it escaped me. You are here with the major?"

The last time I had seen John was on that day which closed the chapter of my happy girlhood in Norfolk. He had been with me when the telegram came telling us that father could not live, and from that day to this I had never seen him until he surprised me patching Dan's old trousers in the cottage at Charlottesville.

He took the chair opposite, and began talking about the work I was doing and the evidence it bore to my being a good wife. But so far from being pleased I was very much mortified, for the old trousers were in a dreadful state of wear and tear, and he was resplendent in a new uniform. But after a while we dropped the trousers, and got on the subject of Norfolk and old times, and had quite a pleasant chat till my husband came in and he and John turned their attention to business.

I was seeing more of my husband than at any previous or later period of the war, and having altogether a delightful time. One of the things I enjoyed most were our horseback rides.

Dan had two horses for his own use Tom Hodges, his old army horse, and Nellie Grey, a fine new mare that he had christened for me. When his horse was shot under him in that charge which has been mentioned before, the people of his native town had sent him Nellie Grey in its stead. Nellie was a beautiful creature, docile but very spirited, and I was not often trusted to ride her unless Dan himself was along. Tom Hodges was not so handsome, but he was a horse of decorous ideas and steadfast principles.

I remember well my first ride on Nellie Grey. I had the reputation of being an excellent horsewoman, and Dan wanted to show me off. He was inordinately proud of me, to my great delight, but I could have dispensed with the form his vanity took on that day.

As we rode in an easy canter down University Avenue he gave Nellie Grey a cut, without my knowledge, that sent her off like the wind in a regular cavalry gallop.

Well, I kept my seat - somehow - and I brought her to her senses and a standstill, and then I looked back to see Dan beaming with pride and pleasure.

"What is the matter with this horse?" I asked. "She's a fool!"

Then Dan told me of that secret cut.

"I knew just what she would do," he said, "and I knew what you'd do. I wanted to show the boys over there what pluck my wife's got."

"Dan," I said solemnly, "it's not Nellie Grey that's the

fool."

I was breathless and vexed, and I had to use the strongest language at my command to express my opinion of Nellie Grey, but it wasn't strong enough to express my feelings toward Dan! I simply had to look my thoughts!

"You see, wifie," he went on apologetically, "you did look so pretty and plucky that you ought to have seen yourself."

Sam had gone home on a furlough, and in his place Dan had a very magnificent body servant named Napoleon Bonaparte, and an under-boy named Solomon. Napoleon Bonaparte brushed the major's boots, and Solomon brushed Napoleon's. Napoleon Bonaparte was a bright mulatto, Solomon was as black as tar. It was Napoleon Bonaparte's business to supply my room with wood, but this task he delegated to Solomon. Whatever menial work the major ordered Napoleon Bonaparte to do, Napoleon turned over to Solomon. "Solomon," he said, "was nothin' but a free nigger nohow." It came to pass finally that Solomon, ostensibly hired to one master, in reality served two. Of course, Napoleon Bonaparte feathered his own nest and worked things so that the major was really paying two men to do the work of one. When the major could not ride with me, he sent Napoleon Bonaparte to act as groom. This Napoleon Bonaparte esteemed an honor, and he only appointed Solomon in his stead when he himself was in demand as equerry for the major. Napoleon always elected to follow the major in such case, as that was higher employment in his eyes than riding behind me. One morning I stood waiting in my habit a long time for the horses. At last when they appeared Solomon came on a sorry mount, leading Tom Hodges. The procession moved at a snail's pace, and Solomon looked dreadfully glum.

"What makes you so late?" I asked impatiently.

"Dunno 'zackly, marm. Evvybody in de camp got de debbul in 'em. Major, he got de debbul in him! 'Poleon

Bonaparte, he got de debbul in him. An' evvybody got de debbul in 'em!"

"There seem to have been a great many devils in camp. Wasn't there one to spare for you, Solomon?"

"Nor'm, I ain't had no debbul in me - me an' Tom Hodges. We's been de onliest peaceable people in camp. Ef I hadn't er kep' de peace, me an' 'Poleon Bonaparte would ha' fit, sho!"

"I should think you would like to fight Napoleon - I should, if I were you."

"Nor'm, I don' b'lieve in no fightin' - 'cep'in' 'tis ter fit de Yankees. I'm er peaceable man, I is."

I told Dan what a bad report Solomon had made out against him.

He laughed. "Solomon has the grumps this morning. He seemed to have quite a time with your namesake, as well as with the rest of us. Napoleon Bonaparte sent him to rub Nellie Grey down and saddle her for me. The mare threw her head up and jerked him about a little, and we could hear him saying: 'Whoa! Nellie Grey, whoa! You got de debbul in you too! Who-a, Nellie Grey!' Between the two of them I am having rather a hard time lately," said Dan. "Solomon blames 'Poleon Bonaparte directly for all the hard times he has, and me indirectly. If something isn't done as it should be, and I take Napoleon to task, he lays it thick and hard on Solomon. Solomon did have a time of it at camp this morning. You see, 'Poleon Bonaparte is very particular about the way the horses are kept, but he makes Solomon do all the rubbing down, and Solomon doesn't understand how to manage horses and is a little afraid of them. 'Poleon Bonaparte found fault with his job this morning, and made him rub Nellie Grey down twice. It naturally occurred to Nellie that so much rubbing meant an opportunity for playing. Black Solomon really was the good angel at camp, for before he and Nellie Grey got us to laughing, swearing had been thick enough to cut with a knife. I had turned loose on 'Poleon, and 'Poleon had turned loose on

Solomon."

"Dan, what makes you keep them both?"

"Keep them both! I don't. I don't want either of them, but I can't get rid of them."

"Make Napoleon do his work and send Solomon off."

"Make! Nell, how you talk! And 'Poleon's got just as much right to hire a nigger as I have to own one."

And during our stay in Charlottesville Dan's servants gave him "more trouble," he said, "than fighting the Yankees." But it was a very happy time in my life.

The late springtime of ' found me again in Petersburg.

More vacant chairs, more broken hearts, more suffering, and starvation nearer at hand was what I found there. Milicent was spending her time in nursing the sick and wounded in the hospital, and winning from them the name that has clung to her ever since. There are old white-haired men in the South who still call her "Madonna."

Chapter XXIII

"Into The Jaws Of Death"

ONE lovely morning mother sat at an upper window shelling peas for dinner. The window commanded a view of the Petersburg heights and beyond. Presently she stopped shelling peas, and gazed intently out of the window.

"What is that on the heights, Nellie?" she asked, and then, "What men are those running about on the hill beyond?"

I came to the window and looked out. The hills looked blue.

With a sinking heart I got the field-glass and turned it southeast. The hills swarmed with soldiers in Federal uniforms! Men in gray were galloping up to the Reservoir and unlimbering guns. We heard the roar of cannon, the rattle of musketry. The heavens were filled with fire and smoke. Men in blue were vanishing as they came; they thought Reservoir Hill a fort. That was the ninth of June, when old men and boys saved the town by holding Kautz's command, , strong, at bay on the Jerusalem Plank Road as long as they could and long enough to give Graham's and Studivant's batteries and Dearing's cavalry time to rush to the front. The Ninth of June is Petersburg's Memorial Day, her day of pride and sorrow.

A few days after - mother was shelling peas again - whiz! whack! a shell sung through the air, striking in Bolling Square. Whiz! whack! came another, and struck Mrs. Dunlop's house two doors from us. Mrs. De Voss, our neighbor on one side, and Mrs. Williams and her two daughters who lived on the other, ran in, pale with terror, and clamored to go down into our cellar. We were like frightened sheep. I half laugh, half cry now with vexation to think how calmly and stubbornly mother sat shelling peas in that window. She was bent on finishing her peas before she moved. Finally we induced her to go with us, and we all went down into the cellar. There we huddled together for the rest of the day, and until late into the night, not knowing what went on above or outside, little Bobby asleep in his mother's lap, and the rest of us too frightened to sleep. At last, when we had heard no guns for a long time, we crept upstairs and lay down on our beds and tried to sleep. The next morning the shelling began again. Shells flew all around us. One struck in the yard next to ours; another horrid, smoking thing dropped in our own yard. We decided that it was time to abandon the house.

As the firing came from the south and the east, and the Appomattox was on the north of the city, we could only turn to the west. Any other direction and we would have run toward the guns or into the river. With no more rhyme or reason than this in our course we started up Washington Street, running west, but without regard to the order of our going.

Crossing the railroad at Jarrett's Hotel, I saw a Confederate soldier whom I recognized as an old playmate and friend of Norfolk days We stopped each other.

"Where did you come from, Harry?"

"Where are you running to, Nell?"

"Why, we were at Miss Anne Walkers and the shells were bursting in our yard, and we are getting out of the way."

Zip! a shell passed over my head and burst a few yards away. I didn't wait to say good-by, but ran along Washington Street for my life. At last we got to Mr. Venable's house, which was out of the range of the guns, and there we stopped with others. Many people had passed us on our way, and we had passed many people, all running through Washington Street for dear life. Everybody seemed to be running; in Mr. Venable's house quite a crowd was gathered. His family were from home, but their friends filled the house. We watched from doors and windows, and talked of our friends who had fallen, of the Ninth of June, and of how Fort Hell and Fort Damnation got their names. We spoke of a friend who had kissed wife and children goodby, and gone out that fateful Ninth with the militia up the Jerusalem Plank Road to Fort Hell. Later in the day a wagon had come lumbering up to the door, blood dripping from it as it jolted along. In it lay the husband and father, literally shot to pieces. His little boy walked weeping behind it. His widow had shrouded him with her own hands, and trimmed his bier herself with the fragrant June flowers that were growing in her yard - flowers which he had loved and helped to tend. She had a house full of little ones around her. She had never known how to work, and now she was going about finding tasks to do, bearing up bravely and strengthening her children, she who had been as dependent upon her husband for love and tenderness as his children were upon her.

As the day waned we saw people hurrying past the Venable home bearing the wounded. I remember one poor fellow who was lying on a stretcher that was borne by his friends. He seemed to be shot almost to pieces. Graycoats were passing now, marching into the city.

As we sat at supper that night - a large party it was at that hospitable board - a servant brought a message to the three of us. A gentleman - a soldier - wished to see us. I went into the hall, and there was Walter Taylor. I don't think I was ever so glad to see anybody in my life. Walter was not only "Walter," but he was General Lee's adjutant, and the very sight of him meant help to us. What did mother, Millie, and I do but throw our arms around his neck and kiss him like crazy women.

"I can't stop a minute," he said. "I heard you were here, and felt that I must come out to see how you were getting along. But I must go straight back to my command. Let me know if I can do anything for you."

"Walter, where is Dan?"

"I don't know, Nell, but I think he will be here to-night -

if he is not here already."

We felt like clinging to Walter and holding him back. I for one had lost my nerve. I was sick of war, sick of the butchery, the anguish, the running hither and thither, the fear. Soon after supper my husband came in. I was tremblingly glad to see him again, to touch his warm living body, to see that he was not maimed and mutilated - yet it hung over me all the time that he must go away, in a few minutes - to come back, or be brought back - how? I kept my hand on him all the time he sat beside me. Every time he moved I trembled, feeling that it was a move to go.

"What are you doing out here?" he asked; "I thought you were at Miss Anne's and went there for you."

"We left there."

"What for?"

"The shells were flying all around us, and we were afraid, and ran out here, I tell you."

"Afraid? Why, Nell, you weren't afraid?"

"Yes, I am - I'm terrified."

"A soldier's wife - a regular campaigner!"

"I can't help it. I'm scared."

"After all you've been through, like the brave girl you are, to break down like a coward!"

"I can't help what you call me, I'm scared - I'm scared to death."

"Nell, I'm ashamed of you."

"I can't help it, Dan; I'm scared."

"What would General Stuart say if he could know?"

"I don't care what he would think. I'm terrified. I'm going to run from those shells as long as there is a place to run to. I'm not going to stand still and let a shell strike me to please anybody. I'm for getting away from town. If I had my way we'd take to the woods this night, and let the Yankees have it."

"They'd mighty soon find us in the woods."

"Then I'd move on. They can have everywhere they come

to now, as far as I am concerned."

Dan looked aghast. I was completely demoralized. Knowing he must go, I summoned all my strength and braced myself for the parting, but though Dan was sorry for me, my effort to be brave was so comical that he had to laugh. By morning the range of the guns was changed, shells were flying all over the city, and our present quarters were not exempt. Zip! zip! crack! bang! the nasty things went everywhere.

We piled ourselves, pell-mell, helter-skelter into the first ambulance we could get and started out Washington Street again as fast as ever we could get the driver to urge his horses.

Everybody was racing out Washington Street, still running west. Pell-mell, helter-skelter, they ran, any way to get out of the range of the horrid, whizzing, singing, zipping bombs. We met Mr. McIlvaine driving toward town, that is, in the direction from which we were running.

He hailed us.

"Where are you going?"

"We don't know where we are going. We are not going anywhere that we know of."

"Go to my house. My family are away, but I can make you welcome. Quite a number of people are out there now."

We found this to be the literal truth. All the floors were covered with mattresses - if you rolled off your own mattress you rolled on to some one else's, for they were laid so thick that they touched. But things might always be worse.

Mr. McIlvaine had an excellent cook. She made delicious rolls and wonderful muffins and wafers, and as far as skill went our provisions were turned into delicious food. There was quite a colony - seven women besides ourselves - and we told Mr. McIlvaine that we could not expect him to feed us all, that we were thankful enough for shelter and to have our cooking done, and that we would all throw in and buy provisions. So we made a common fund, and sent for such things as could be had by Mr. McIlvaine whenever he went into town.

My husband came out to see me quite often during the weeks that followed, and Colonel Taylor and many of our military friends remembered us by dropping in to tea and spending an evening with us when they could. There was a piano in the parlor, and our evenings were often gay with singing, music, and dancing. There was but one servant on the place as I remember - the cook I have spoken of, and whom I remember vividly and affectionately for the good things to eat she set before us. To cook for us, however, was about all she could do. We had but few clothes with us, and when these got soiled there was no washerwoman to be had, so when Sue Williams said she was going to wash her clothes herself we all got up our washings, and went down into the back yard with her. We found some tubs and drew our water, and made up some fire under a pot, as we had seen the negroes do. I can see Sue now, drawing water and lifting buckets back and forth from the well. We tied some clothes up in a sheet and put them into the pot to boil; then we put some other clothes in a tub and began to wash; meanwhile we had to keep up the fire under the pot. It was dinner hour by the time we got thus far. The weather was very hot and we were dreadfully tired, and we hadn't got any clothes on the line yet. We stopped to swallow our dinner, and went at it again. The sun was going down when we had a pile of clothes washed, rinsed, and wrung, ready for the line. We didn't know what to do about it. There didn't seem to be any precedent that we had ever known for hanging clothes out at sundown. On the other hand, if we didn't spread them out they would mildew - we had heard of such things. If they had to be spread out, certainly there was no better place to spread them than on the line. So at sunset we hung out our clothes to dry. There were handkerchiefs on the line and a petticoat apiece. The rest of the clothes were in the pot and the tub, and they are there now for aught I know to the contrary. I don't know what became of them, but I know we went into the house and went to bed with the backache and every other sort of ache. I have never in all my life worked so hard as I worked that day trying to wash my clothes out; and the next day the clothes on the line looked yellow for all the labor that was put upon them. I have never known why they looked yellow - not for lack of work, for we had rubbed holes in some of them. We did not undertake to iron them for fear we should make them look still worse, but wore them rough dry.

Early one morning we waked suddenly, and sprang to our feet and reached for each other's trembling hands. There had been a sudden and terrific noise. The earth was shaking. That awful thunder! that horrible quaking of the earth! as if its very bowels were being rent asunder! What was it? We tried to whisper to each other through the darkness of our rooms, but our tongues were dry and palsied with fear. We feared to draw the curtains of our windows, we dared not move. That was the morning of the th of July, the morning when the Crater was made when an entire regiment was blown into the air, and when into the pit left behind them Federals and Confederates marched over each other, and fought all day like tigers in a hole. If you ever go to the quaint old town of Petersburg, you can drive out the old Jerusalem Plank Road to Forts Hell and Damnation, and you can turn out of it to a large hole in the earth which is called the Crater. The last time I was at the Crater it was lined with grass; some sassafras bushes grew on the sides; down in the hollow was a peach-tree in blossom, a mocking-bird sang in it, and a rabbit hopped away as I looked down.

Soon after the explosion occurred, we saw from our windows that the McIlvaine place was swarming with soldiers who were throwing up earthworks everywhere. They were our own soldiers, of course, and we applied for an ambulance and got one, and went back in it to Miss Anne's in town.

I shall never forget how that deserted house felt when we three women and little Bobby entered it. The dust was on everything and there was a musty smell about everywhere.

That night Millie had high fever. Such a wretched night as it was! no servants, no conveniences, little or no food Millie in a raging fever, little sleepy Bobby crying for his mother and his supper; the shock of the Crater still upon us, danger underneath, overhead, everywhere. The next morning Millie's fever was lower, and she seemed better.

"We must get her away from here, of she will die," mother said.

But how? We could hear nothing of Dan and didn't know where to find him. Mother sent a note to General Mahone by a passing soldier asking for a pass to Richmond. Her reply was an ambulance and a driver who brought a note from the general, saying that we would be taken outside of the city to the nearest point to where our trains from Richmond were allowed to come. We got Millie into the ambulance and were taken to the Dunlops', a beautiful place on the Richmond Railroad. Here we waited for a train which did not come. Night came on; still we waited, but no train. We sent into the house and asked for lodgings. Answer came that the house was full, and no more people could be taken in. Millie's fever continued to rise. We sent again, saying how ill she was, and begging for shelter for the night. The same answer was returned, and there we were out on the lawn, our shawls spread on two trunks and Millie lying on them, and looking as if every breath would be her last.

"Do you know where Colonel Walter Taylor is stationed?" I asked our driver.

"Yes, ma'am. I know exactly where he is. His camp is about a mile from here."

"How could I get a note to him?"

"I will go with it. I'll take one of the horses out of the ambulance."

I scratched off:

"DEAR WALTER: We are out in the woods near Dunlop's without any shelter, and Millie is very ill. Can you help us?

"Affectionately,

"NELL."

The driver took the note and Walter came back with him.

"I don't know what to do, Nell," he said. "There is no train to Richmond till noon to-morrow, but you can't stay out here."

He went himself to the house, but without effect.

"I will send you a tent and a doctor," he said.

"That is the best I can do for you. I wish I could stay here with you all and help take care of Millie to-night, but I must go back at once."

The tent came and with it Dr. Newton, ad Millie was made as comfortable as was possible on the trunks.

An old negress who was passing saw our strait and brought us her pillow in a clean pillow-case, and we put that under Millie's head. We gave "aunty" some tea that we had with us, and she took it to her cabin and drew us a cup or two over her fire, and we got Millie to swallow a little of it. We picked Bobby up off the grass, and dropped him on a pile of bags in a corner of the tent.

At one time that night we thought Millie would die - the doctor himself was doubtful if she could live till morning. When morning came she was alive, and that was all. Dr. Newton sent for a stretcher and had her lifted on it into the train. That was a terrible journey; there were many delays, and we thought we should never get to Richmond, but we were there at last. We went into the waiting-room at the station and sent for Major Grey's brother. Fortunately, he was quickly found, and took us to the house at which he boarded and where there was a vacant room. The city was crowded, and on such short notice it was the best he could do, but it was stifling little place.

The room was small, its only window opened on a little dark hallway, there was an objectionable closet attached to the room, and the close, unwholesome air made me sick and faint as we opened the door. We laid Millie on the bed. Suddenly she gasped, moaned something that sounded like "I am dying!" and seemed to be dead.

"Air!" cried mother hopelessly, "she needs air."

But there was no window for Dick to throw up.

He picked her up in his arms, ran down the steps with her, and into the open street. The ladies in the house all came out to us, offering help and sympathy, and with us got Millie into the parlor, where we laid her on a lounge, and where two physicians worked over her for hours before they were sure she would recover entirely from the attack. They said it was heart failure. That evening we carried her on a stretcher to the Spotswood Hotels. She was ill for two weeks. Then Bobby was ill for five. Our funds ran out. What moneys we had were in the Yankee lines and inaccessible, and Millie determined to put her education and accomplishments to use. She set herself to work to find something to do, and a lady from Staunton who happened to meet us at this time, learning that she wanted work, offered her a position in a young ladies' school. So Lillie and little Bobby went to Staunton.

Chapter XXIV

By The Skin Of Our Teeth

NOT long after they left, mother and I came in from a round of calls one day to find a telegram awaiting me:

"Dan wounded, but not dangerously. Come.

"Gus."

I hurried into my room and changed my dress - to be careful of wearing apparel had become a pressing necessity - while mother went out to see about trains. We found there was no Petersburg train till next day; there might be one at seven in the morning. I was up at daybreak, got a cup of tea and a biscuit, looked at mother as she lay asleep, and with my satchel and little lunch basket in my hand went to the depot. There were crowds of soldiers there and a train about to start, but no woman was to go on it - it was for soldiers only. I went from one person who seemed to be in authority to another, seeking permission to go, but received the same answer everywhere - only soldiers were allowed on the train.

"But," I said at last, "I am an officer's wife, and he is wounded." I broke down with the words, and in spite of my efforts to keep them back my eyes filled with tears. I was what I should have done in the beginning. I at once got permission. I went into the car, took my seat at the extreme end and shrunk into the smallest space possible. The car was packed with soldiers and I was the only woman on board. When we were about half-way a young lieutenant who occupied part of the seat in front of me said:

"Madam, if I can be of any assistance to you, please command me. I suppose you know that our train stops within three miles of Petersburg."

"I did not know," I said, "and I do not know what to expect, or what I shall do, or where I shall find my husband, although I suppose I shall be met."

"If not," he said, "I am at your service."

No one was waiting for me at the depot; but the lieutenant secured an ambulance, got in it with me, and directed the driver to take us to Petersburg. We soon met Gus, Dan's cousin, coming to meet me in a buggy. While I was getting out of the ambulance into the buggy I was plying Gus with questions about Dan. "Dan is at our house," Gus told me. "His wound is a very ugly one, but the doctors say that he'll get well. At first we thought he wouldn't. He is shot through the thigh, and will be laid up for some time - that's what he's kicking about now."

Our most direct route to Mansfield, where Dan was, lay through Petersburg, but we could not follow that route. The Yankees were everywhere about the city, Gus said, so we went through the outer edge of Ettricks, skirting the city proper. When we reached Mansfield my husband on crutches met me at the door. He looked pale and weak, but he was very cheery and tried to joke.

"He ought not to have got up, Nell," whispered Grandmamma Grey. "He thought it would shock you to find him in bed - that is why he got up."

Of course I immediately put him under orders. He returned to bed meekly enough, and from that time I did all I could, and it was all I could do, to keep him still until his wound healed. We read and sang and played on the banjo and had a good time. But as soon as he was able to hobble he would go to camp every day and sit around. General Lee's headquarters were about a mile and a half from our house. Colonel Taylor and a number of old friends were there, and Dan could talk fight if he couldn't fight. At last he insisted that he was ready to join his division, and we set out to reach it in an ambulance drawn by three mules.

When we came to Hatchers Run we found that creek very much swollen and the bridge not visible, but there were fresh tracks showing where a wagon had lately gone over.

"That shows well enough where the bridge is," said Dan, pointing to where the wagon had left a track close to the water's edge and visible for a short way under the water. "Follow that track," he commanded our drivers who was three-quarters of a man, being too young for a whole man and too old for a lad, "the mules will find the bridge. They are the most sure-footed animals in the world. Just let them have their heads as soon as they get in the water."

Jerry obeyed instructions. Sure enough, the mules got along well enough. That is, for a short distance. Then, splash! down they went under the water! We could just see their noses and their great ears wiggling above the surface as they struck out into a gallant swim for the opposite shore. Splash! we went in after them, and mules and ambulance were swimming and floating together. Jerry was terrified, and began to pray so hard that I got to laughing. All we could see of the mules were six ears sticking out of the water and wiggling for dear life, while our ambulance swam along like a gondola.

But things changed suddenly. Our ambulance was lifted slightly, came down with a jolt, and wouldn't budge! The mules strained forwards but to no good. The ambulance wouldn't stir, and their harness held them back. "The ambulance has caught on some part of the bridge," said Dan.

We were in a serious dilemma. The road was one in much use, and we pinned our hopes to some passer-by, but as we waited minutes seemed hours. No one came. Perhaps the wagon that had preceded us had given warning that the bridge was wrecked. We sat in the ambulance and waited, not knowing what to do, not seeing what we could do. By some saplings which stood in the water we measured the rise of the tide, and we measured its rise in the ambulance by my trunk - I was getting wet to my knees. Finally I sat on top of my trunk and drew my feet up after me. The situation was serious enough, and Dan began to look very anxious - Hatchers Run was always regarded as a dangerous stream in flood time. Still, no sign of any one coming. The rain continued to fall and the water to rise.

"At this rate we are sitting here to drown," Dan said. "There's but one way out of it that I can see. From what I know of the situation of our army there must be an encampment near here. Jerry, climb out of this ambulance over the backs of these hind mules till you get to that leader. Get on him, cut him loose, and swim out of this. Ride until you find an encampment and bring us help."

But Jerry didn't look at it that way.

"I'm skeered ter fool 'long dat ar mule. I ain't nuvver fooled 'long er mule in de water. I kaint have no notion of de way he mought do wid me. You kaint 'pend on mules, Mars Dan, ter do jes lak you want 'em ter on dry land, much less in de water. Arter I git out dar, cut dat ar mule loose, an' git on him, he mought take out an' kyar me somewhar I didn't wanter go. I mought nuvver git ter no camp, nor nowhar, Mars Dan, ef I go ter foolin' 'long er dat mule out dar in de water."

The major caught his shoulders, and turned his face to the stream. "Have you watched that water rising out there for nothing?" he asked sternly. "We are sure to be drowned if you don't do as I tell you - all of us."

Between certain death and uncertain death Jerry chose the latter, crawled over the hind mules, got on the leader and rode him off. He took this note with him:

"Nearest Encampment of any Division, C. S. A.: "I am in the middle of Hatchers Run in an ambulance with my wife. The stream is rising rapidly and ambulance filling with water. Send immediate relief.

"DANIEL V. GREY, "Adjutant of the Thirteenth."

After the boy was gone there we sat and waited while the water rose. I got very cold and Dan, who was yet weak from his wound and confinement, got chilled and stiff. After more than an hour of waiting we heard from the woods on the other side a noise as of men running, and then there came rushing out of the woods toward us thirteen men of mighty girth and stature. They were Georgia mountaineers who had been sent to our rescue. When they came to the water they didn't like the look and feel of it, and evidently didn't want to get in it.

"What is we uns to do?" they called across. "Something to get us out of this," Dan hallooed back, "and be quick about it, or we shall drown."

"How is we uns to git to you uns?"

"Get in the water and swim here."

They talked among themselves, but none of them seemed disposed to do this.

"Men!" called my husband, "I am hardly well of a wound, I am stiff and weak. I can not save my wife, who is up to the waist in water. Will you stand there and see a woman drown?"

They seemed ashamed, but none of them made the move to go in. Then the largest of them all - he seemed a mighty giant - stepped forth and took command.

"You say thar's a lady in that ambulance?"

"Yes, my wife."

"Wall, I'm blowed! An' she ain't a-hollerin' and a-cryin'?"

"Do you hear her?" asked Dan irritably. "She's braver than some men I know. But you can count on it that she is wet and cold. We are nearly frozen!"

"Wall, I'm blowed! An' she's right out thar in the middle er that run, an' she ain't a-hollerin' and a-cryin'! Tell you uns what I'll do. I'll swim out there and bring her back on my back. An' then I'll swim back agin an' bring you on my back."

"I can't!" I said. "I'm cold enough to die now, and I can't get in that water. I'll die if I do."

The giant gave orders. The men hung back. Then we

heard him roaring like a bull of Bashan.

"Git into that ar water, evvy man of you uns, an' swim fur that ar ambulance! I was put in comman' er this here expuddition, an' means ter comman' it. 'Bey orders, you uns is got ter, or you uns 'll git reported to headquarters ez I'm a sinner. Git in that :har water. Furrard! Swim!"

How well I remember the great, good natured giant as he swam around our ambulance, bobbing up and down, and taking n our bearings!

"You see, cap," he said, "all the bridge is washed away but the sleepers, an' that's what you uns is hung on. Unhitch them mules," to some of his men.

"Now, cap, soon's them mules is loose we uns 'll lif' the ambulance off er this, an' pull you uns to shore. Jes you uns make yourse'fs easy, and we uns 'll git you uns out er this."

The mules unhitched were led to shore, and then the men pulled the ambulance safely to land. I don't remember what became of the thirteen mighty men. Nor do I recall clearly the rest of that cold ride when I shivered in my clothes, but I remember getting to a house where I was seated in a great chair close to a blazing fire of hickory logs, and I remember that when I went to get out my night-dress I found all the clothes in my trunk wet, and that when I went to bed I felt as if I were going to be ill, and that I rested badly. But the next morning I was up and on my way again. Again we came to a swollen stream. This time we could see the bridge, and it wobbled about. Dan thought it was safe to drive over. But not I! Just then some gentlemen came up behind us and insisted that I was right. So I got out of the ambulance and was helped across on some logs or beams or something which stretched across the stream underneath the bridge, and may have been a part of it, but whatever they were I thought them more secure than an ambulance and mules and an uncertain bridge. I made Dan cross this way, too, though he said it wasn't best for his leg, and made all sorts of complaints about it. The ambulance was obliged to cross on the bridge, and the devoted Jerry drove it, quarreling and complaining and praying all the way. We had not gone much farther before, lo! here was Stony Creek, swollen to bursting, rushing and furious, and again a hidden bridge.

"I nuvver seed so much high water befo' in all my life," said Jerry, thoroughly disgusted, "nor so dang'ous. Water behin' an' befo'. We all is in a bad way."

There was a wagoner on the bank who said the bridge was all right and but slightly under water. I protested, but Dan made Jerry drive in. I wanted to turn back. But Dan argued that there was as bad behind us, and that he must get to camp by the time he was due, and after a little the mules found their footing and kept it, though the water swished and whirled over the bridge. We saw a man and a horse swept down the stream - I thought they might have been swept by the current off the very bridge we were crossing. The current was too strong for the horse; he could do nothing against it, and had given up. As they passed under a tree the man reached up, caught a sweeping branch and swung himself up in the tree; the horse was drowned before our eyes before we got across the bridge.

We left the man in the tree, but promised to send him help. There was a house two miles from the creek, and to this we drove. It was full of people; the parlor was full, the halls were full, and the kitchen and the bedrooms were full of men, women, and children. It reminded me of a country funeral where people are piled up in the halls, on the steps, and everywhere a person can stand or sit. Soldiers were always passing to and fro in those days and stopping for the night at any convenient wayside place, and as for not taking a soldier in - well, public opinion made it hot for the man who would not shelter a wayfaring soldier and share the last crust with him. The house held a large number of soldiers that night, and in addition a water-bound wedding-party. On this side the creek was the groom; on the other side the bride. The groom had on his good clothes - good clothes were a rarity then - but he looked most woebegone. We told the people in the house about the man in the tree; and every man in the house went down to see about him.

They called out to him saying they would throw him ropes and pull him in, but when they tried to throw the ropes out to him they found that he could not be reached in that way. The tree was too far from the shore. It was after midnight when they gave up trying to reach him with ropes. Then they told him to keep his courage up till morning, and they made a great bonfire on the banks, and some of them stood by it and talked to him all night. First one party and then another would go out and stand by the bonfire, and keep it up, and talk to him. The relieved party would come to the house and warm themselves and go back again. Nobody slept that night. There was nowhere for anybody to lie down. When morning came the creek had fallen and they pulled the nearly frozen man to land.

The next day found us at our destination, Hicksford.

Chapter XXV

THE BEGINNING OF THE END

WHILE I was at Hicksford I stayed at General Chambliss's. I was very happy there. Dan's camp was not far off, and he came to see me very often and every morning sent his horses to me. In my rides I used frequently to take the general's little son, Willie, along as my escort, and one morning, when several miles distant from home and with our horses' heads turned homeward, who should ride out from a bend in the road and come toward us but two full-fledged Yankees in blue uniform and armed to the teeth. My heart went down into the bottom of my horse's heels, and I suppose Willie's heart behaved the same way. We did not speak, we hardly breathed, and we were careful not to quicken our pace as we and our enemies drew nearer and nearer, and passed in that lonely road a yard between our horses and theirs.

We did not turn back; we crept along the road to the bend, until our horses' tails got well around the bend. Then Willie and I gave each other a look, and took out at a wild run for home. We went straight as arrows, and over everything in our way. I had all I could do that day to stick on Nellie Grey, who went as if she knew Yankees were behind - only in her mind it must have been the whole of Grant's army. Dan laughed our "narrow escape" to scorn, and said the two Yankees were probably Confederates in good Yankee clothes they had confiscated. At this time Confederates would put on anything they found to wear, from a woman's petticoat to a Yankee uniform, but Dan never could convince us that those two

Yankees were not Yankees.

After this I rebelled less against going out, as I sometimes had to do, in "Miss Sally's kerridge." This was an old family carriage, a great coach of state with the driver's perch very high. The driver, an old family negro as venerable and shaky in appearance as the carriage, attached due importance to his office. He thought no piece of furniture on the place of such value as "Miss Sally's kerridge." He cared for the horses as if they had been babies. This part of the country had not been so heavily taxed as some others in the support of the two armies, and a little more corn than was usual could be had. Uncle Rube was sure that his horses got the best of what was going, and also that everything a currycomb could do for them was theirs. He himself when prepared for his post as charioteer wore a suit of clothes which must have been in the Chambliss family for several generations, and an old beaver hat, honorable with age and illustrious usage. When we were taken abroad in "Miss Sally's kerridge," we were always duly impressed by Uncle Rube with the honor done us. On the occasion of a grand review which took place not far from General Chambliss's residence, I, with three other ladies, went in the "kerridge." The roads were awful - in those days roads were always awful. Troops were traveling backward and forward, artillery was being dragged over them, heavy wagons were cutting ruts, and there always seemed to be so much rain.

Uncle Rube quarreled all the way going and coming. He sat on his high perch, and guided his horses carefully along, picking the best places in the road for "Miss Sally's kerridge," and talking at us.

"It's jes gwine to ruin Miss Sally's kerridge takin' it out on sech roads as dese hyer. . . . Nuf to ruin er ox-kyart, dese hyer roads is, much mo'er fin' kerridge. . . . Well, 'tain' no use fur me ter say nothin'. . . . Jest well keep my mouf shut. . . . Monstratin' don' do er bit er good . . . . When dey git it in dar haids dey's gwine, dey's gwine, don't kyeer what happens . . . . Ain't gwine heah nothin', dey ain't, not ontwell dey gits Miss Sally's kerridge broke up. . . . I say folks orter go ter ride when de roads is good, and stay at home when de roads is bad. . . . An' lemme take kyeer uv de kerridge."

With these intermittent mutterings and frank expressions of displeasure Uncle Rube entertained us until we got to the review stand.

To crown his disgust we were late in starting back home, and at dark he was leaning forward from his lofty altitude, peering into the road ahead and seeking vainly "de bes' place ter drive Miss Sally's kerridge along." He said "dar warn't no bes' place," and was in despair of ever getting that valuable vehicle home in safety. At last the crash came! Down went one carriage wheel into a mud-hole! It stuck there, and we were rooted for the time being. However, I think Uncle Rube would have got us out but for some untimely assistance. Bob Lee, the youngest of the Lees, and Bob Mason (the son of the ex-United States Minister to France, whose home was near General Chambliss's) came riding by. They stopped and shook hands with us through the carriage window, and asserted their gallant intention of getting us out of our mud-hole. They tried to leads the horses forward, to pull and push "the kerridge" out, but in vain. Then Bob, to Uncle Rube's utter amazement and indignation, made him get down, while he, Bob, mounted the box. Uncle Rube stood on the roadside, the picture of chagrin and despair.

"Dar ain't no tellin' what's gwi' happen now!" he exclaimed. "Mars Bob don' know how ter manage dem horses no mo'n nothin'. Don', Mars Bob! Mars Bob! don' whoop 'em! Law-aw-dy!"

Bob had gathered the lines in one hand and with the other was laying the whip on Rube's pets. The horses, utterly unused to the whip, plunged like mad. There was an ominous sound! - our axle was broken, and we were helplessly stuck in the mud.

"Dar now!" wailed Uncle Rube. "What I tole you? I said

Miss Sally's kerridge gwi' git ruint! and now it's done been did. It's clean ruint, Miss Sally's kerridge is. I tole Mars Bob dem horses don't know nothin' 'bout a whoop. Dey ain't nuvver bin 'quainted wid er whoop. I bin er-sayin' an' er-sayin' all erlong dat de kerridge gwi' git broke, an' it's done been did. O Lawdy!"

Our young rescuers borrowed a cart from a farmer near by and got us home in it. I have forgotten how Uncle Rube managed, if I ever knew. But I shall never forget the scene when several hours later we all sat around the fire in the sitting-room, chatting over our adventures, and Uncle Rube, hat in hand, came to the door and made report to his mistress of the family misfortune. His eyes were big as saucers. He laid the blame thick and heavy on "Mars Bob's" shoulders, exonerating his horses with great care.

"Dey's sensubble horses ef anybody jes got de sense ter manage 'em, dey is."

And then Miss Sally, in spite of her efforts to preserve a gravity befitting the calamity, broke down like the "kerridge" and laughed hysterically.

There was plenty to eat at General Chambliss's. I always remember that fact when it was a fact, because it was beginning to be so pleasant and unusual to have enough to eat. Hicksford hadn't been raided, and there were still chickens on the roost, bees in the hive, turkeys up the trees, partridges in the woods, and corn in the barns. The barn, by the way, was new, and the soldiers gave a ball in it. We all went and had a most delightful evening. I well remember that I went in "Miss Sally's kerridge," and that General Rooney Lee and I led off the ball together. I remember, too, that we had a fine supper: turkeys, chicken-salad, barbecued mutton, roast pig with an apple in his mouth, pound-cake, silver-cake, cheese-cake or transparent pudding, "floating island" or "tipsy squire"; plenty of bread, milk, sure-enough coffee - everything and enough of it. We danced till morning and leaving our gallant entertainers in the gray dawn, went off to sleep nearly all day.

The next ball was in an old farmhouse where some of our cavalry were quartered. We had another good supper - everything good to eat and plenty of it - like the first. There were no chairs or furniture of any kind, as I remember, but there were benches ranged around the barn for us to sit on when resting during the pauses of the dance. After a dance with him General Rooney Lee led me back to the room where the banquet was spread to taste something especially nice which he liked and which I had not touched - eating a good thing when you could get it was a delightful and serious duty in those days. There was quite a circle around us, and we were all nibbling, laughing, chatting away as if there were no such things as war and death in the land, when a courier in muddy boots strode across the room to the general, saluted, spoke a few words, and the general walked aside with him. The music was enticing, and while the general was engaged with the courier I went back with some one else to the ballroom and took my place in the lancers. We were clasping hands and bowing ourselves through the grand chain when the dance was interrupted. The army was to march.

There was great confusion, hurried handshaking, sometimes no hand-shaking at all, no time for good-bye. The soldiers could not stand on the order of their going. I do not remember how I came to the farmhouse, but I know that my husband bundled me unceremoniously into a cart with some people I hardly knew, and sent me home, telling me to pack my trunk but not to be disappointed if he could not take me with him. I did not lie down at all. I packed my trunk as soon as I got home, then sat down and waited, and before long my husband came for me in an ambulance. His courier, Lieutenant Wumble, was with him, and the ambulance was driven by an Irishman named Miles. The horses were tied to the back of the ambulance, and frequently my husband and Lieutenant Wumble rode ahead reconnoitering. It began to rain. "What made you always start in the rain?" I have been asked by friends to whom I was relating my campaigns. What I want to know is, what made it always rain when I started? Let me but step into an ambulance and immediately it began to rain. My movements had to be regulated by the movements of the army, not by the weather, though really the weather seemed to regulate itself by mine.

We found the roads worse as we advanced. The farther we went the deeper was the mud. Mud came up to the hubs of our wheels; the mules could hardly pull their feet up out of the miry mass in some places. At last we found ourselves regularly "stuck in the mud." There was no pushing or pulling the ambulance farther. It was nearly dark, but fortunately we were near a farmhouse, and at the side of the road where we got stuck was a stile made by blocks of unequal heights set on either side of a plank fence. These blocks were simply sections of the round body of a tree which had been sawed up. On the opposite side of the stile a pathway led to the house. The mud-hole in which our ambulance was embedded was about ten yards from the stile. My husband insisted that I be carried bodily to the stile, and Lieutenant Wumble, who was one of the most gallant fellows in the world, took it as a matter of course that he must carry me. He urged that he had been brought along to be useful and that Dan had never recovered entirely from his wound. But Dan hooted at the idea! He was very much obliged to the lieutenant, but really he was used to this sort of thing, and understood lifting ladies about much better than Wumble. It was not altogether brute strength, but some science that was required. So Dan stepped out of the ambulance on to the side of the mud-hole, where of course the ground was not so muddy as in the center where we were stuck, but where it was rather slippery, nevertheless. Balancing himself nicely, he took me out, but just as he poised me on his arm with scientific ease and grace he slipped and fell backward, sprawling in the mud, and I went over his head, sprawling, too.

Whereupon Lieutenant Wumble, laughing, came to pick me up, saying as he did so:

"I told you that you ought to let me carry you. Just lie there, major, and I'll come back for you as soon as I set your wife down. Keep quiet, major," as Dan swore at the mud and slipped again, "and I'll pick you up and get you along all right."

As Dan dragged himself up he was a perfect mud man, and he had left the print of himself in the mud behind him. They took us in at the farmhouse, and sent men to help the driver prize the ambulance out of the hole. They scraped the mud off me, and a colored woman washed my clothes and hung them by the fire, so they might be dry by morning. Of course, this process put me in bed at once. Our supper was poor and the bed uncomfortable, but it was the best our hosts could do.

After an uncomfortable night we started off again toward Dinwiddie Court-house, which was to be our next stopping-place. As we journeyed on we knew that we were getting into most dangerous quarters. The nearer we drew to Petersburg the nearer we were to the tangle of Federal and Confederate lines; the nearer to skirmishers and scouts from both armies. The night got blacker and blacker - you could not see your hand before you - and the blacker it grew the more frightened old Miles became. Out of the darkness where, invisible, he sat astride the invisible mule he drove, he poured an unceasing stream of complaint.

"Arrah! the divil a bit can Oi see where Oi'm goin'. It's so dark ye couldn't see a light if there was any. The mules, intilligint crathurs they are, maybe they know where they be goin'. It's more than the loikes of me does. But what Oi've got agin a mule is that they don't know an honest Amerikin in gray clothes - or mixed rags it is now - from a nasty, thavin' Yankee."

If we were silent for a few minutes, then Miles spoke out for company's sake, or asked unnecessary questions perhaps to find out if we were there, and that the Yankees hadn't spirited us away.

"These woods are full of Yankees," he said. "It's chock-full of them, it is. An' it's so dark, it is, they could just come out here an' kill us all, they could, an' we'd never know it."

"Shut your mouth up, you fool!" said my husband, who knew that the woods were full of Yankees. "If we can't see them they can't see us, and how are they to know but we are Yankees unless you tell them, you blathering idiot?"

"The divil a bit Oi'll be tellin' 'em, the nasty blue thaves. Thrust Miles O'Flannigan for thet. But they could just come out o' them woods, they could, an' take us all prisoners an' we'd never know it. An' the driver's the fust man they'd git, sure."

At last Dan got out, mounted his horse, and rode in front of the ambulance.

"Now," said he to Miles, "follow me, and if you open your d - mouth again, I'll blow your brains out."

Lieutenant Wumble brought up the rear, riding behind the ambulance with a cocked pistol. And so we rode through the Egyptian darkness of the night, and the now more than Egyptian silence. Miles's mouth was effectually closed. He followed Dan, whom he could not see, by the sound of his horse's tread, and as he was careful to keep as close to him as possible we made better progress.

We had been in the darkness so long that none of us knew our whereabouts. Presently we heard the low, deep mutterings of thunder. It came nearer and grew louder rapidly. Suddenly the sky seemed rent! There came a sheet of white lightning and with it an awful crash which made my heart stand still. A tree a few feet from us had been struck. The lightning had shown us that we were only a few miles from the Court-house. I have never known such a storm as the one through which we traveled that night. One peal of thunder did not die away before another began. One instant we were in thick darkness - a darkness that could be felt - the next, ourselves, the woods, the road, were bathed in a fierce white light. Between the Yankees and the storm that night I think

Miles would have become a gibbering idiot but for the equalizing influence of Dan's pistol.

"No trouble for the Yankees to rickonize us - ugh!" the rest of the sentence would be lost in the darkness, but I knew that Miles was feeling the salutary muzzle of Dan's pistol against some part of his face.

By the time we entered the village the storm had abated. We drove to the hotel. It was crowded, packed with soldiers; no room for us, nor food either, and nine o'clock at night!

"Two miles the other side of town there is a place of entertainment where you can be accommodated, I think," the hotel proprietor told Dan.

"I don't go any farther to-night with my wife," Dan said resolutely.

"It's not mesilf as wants to be traveling any farther either," Miles put in. "It's divil a bit of a pleasure ride Oi'm havin'."

He was promptly silenced, and was made to drive us around to the various places in the village that had been mentioned; and in spite of the discouragements received, he added his earnest solicitations to ours that we might be lodged for the night. But in spite of our own pleas and Miles's eloquence, midnight found us out at the two-miles place. I don't know how long it had taken us to make those two miles. We had toiled over muddy roads, through fierce extremes of light and darkness, and amid deafening thunder, for the storm had come on again with renewed fury and was at its height when we stopped at the house to which we had been directed. In response to my husband's knock an old man came to the door - the meanest old man I have ever seen before or since. He said we couldn't come in, there wasn't standing room in the house, the house was full of soldiers. My husband said he would come in - that he had a lady with him. I think he would have shot that old man then and there rather than have carried me farther. But the old man said if he had a lady with him all the more reason why he should not come in; the soldiers were drinking, and he whispered to Dan, and I saw Dan give in. He told Dan that he had a cousin in the village who would house us, and he directed us how to get to this cousin's house, so we turned and drove back to the village we had just left. We made better time on our return, as we were better directed and took a shorter route, found the house to which we had been sent, and were taken in.

It was a strange old house, built in colonial days, with the veranda that ran all around it supported by tall Corinthian columns. We woke the owner up - an old man, who came down to the door shivering, candle in hand, and led us through a latticed room, then into another room and up a narrow flight of stairs with sharp turns to a bedroom with dormer windows and ancient furniture. We were welcome to our lodgings, he said, but he had nothing to eat in the house - we would be welcome to it if he had. He looked gaunt and hungry himself.

We had no fire. He left us his candle and went down in the dark himself and we got to bed as quickly as possible. Lieutenant Wumble, who was down-stairs looking after Miles and the horses and the mules, got himself stowed away somewhere.

Next morning my husband was ill; but the old man's wife gave him some of her remedies, and with the help of a little money from me got something for us all to eat. About noon Dan insisted that he was able to travel, and that he must reach his command that day. When we arrived at Petersburg my husband put me on the train for Richmond and bade me goodby. It was the last time I saw him before the surrender.

Chapter XXVI

How We Lived In The Last Days Of The Confederacy

THOUGH the last act of our heroic tragedy was already beginning I was so far from suspecting it that I joined mother at the Arlington, prepared to make a joke of hardships and wring every possible drop of pleasure out of a winter in Richmond, varied, as I fondly imagined, by frequent if brief visits from Dan.

The Arlington was kept on something like the European plan, not from choice of landlady or guests but from grim necessity. Feeding a houseful of people was too arduous and uncertain an undertaking in those days for a woman to assume. Mrs. Fry, before our arrival in July, had informed her boarders that they could continue to rent their rooms from her, but that they must provide their own meals. We paid her $ a month for our room - the price of a house in good times and in good money. During my absence in Mansfield, Hicksford, and other places, mother, to reduce expenses, had rented half of her room and bed to Delia McArthur, of Petersburg. I now rented a little bed from Mrs. Fry for myself, and set it up in the same room.

We had become so poor and had so little to cook that we did most of our cooking ourselves over the grate, each woman often , cooking her own little rations. There was an old negress living in the back yard who cooked for any or all of us when we had something that could not be prepared by ourselves over the grate. Sometimes we got hold of a roast, or we would buy two quarts of flour, a little dab of lard, and a few pinches of salt and treat ourselves to a loaf of bread, which the old negress cooked for us, charging ten dollars for the baking. But as a rule the grate was all sufficient. We boiled rice or dried apples or beans or peas in our stew-pan, and we had a frying-pan if there was anything to fry.

Across the hall from us Miss Mary Pagett, of Petersburg, had a room to herself. She worked in one of the departments, and in order that she might have her meals in time she went into partnership with us. Every morning she would put in with our rations whatever she happened to have for that day, and mother would cook it and have it ready when she came. Down-stairs under our room Mr. and Mrs. Sampson, their daughters Nan and Beth, and their son Don, all of Petersburg and old neighbors and friends of ours, lived, slept, cooked, and ate in two rooms, a big and a little one. They lived as we did, cooking over their grates.

Sometimes we all put what we had together and ate in company. When any of us secured at any time some eatable out of the common, if it was enough to go around we invited the others into breakfast, dinner, or tea, as the case might be. It must be understood that from the meal called "tea," the beverage from which the meal is named was nearly always omitted. Our fare was never very sumptuous - often it was painfully scanty. Sometimes we would all get so hungry that we would put together all the money we could rake and scrape and buy a bit of roast or something else substantial and have a feast.

We all bought coal in common. Mother's, mine, and Delia's portion of the coal was a ton, and we had to keep it in our room - there was no other place to store it. We had a box in our room which held a ton, and the coal was brought up-stairs and dumped into that box. I can see those darkies now, puffing and blowing, as they brought that coal up those many steps. And how we had to scuffle around to pay them! For some jobs we paid in trade - only we had very little to trade off. How that room held all its contents I can't make out. Dan sent me provisions by the quantity when he could get any and get them through to me. He would send a bag of potatoes or peas, and he never sent less than a firkin of butter - delicious butter from Orange County. The bags of peas, rice, and potatoes were disposed around the room, and around the hearth were arranged our pots, pans, kettles, and cooking utensils generally. When we bought wood that was put under the beds. In addition to all our useful and ornamental articles we had our three selves and our trunks; such clothing as we possessed had to be hung up for better keeping - and this was a time when it behooved us to cherish clothes tenderly. Then there was our laundrying, which was done in that room by ourselves.

And we had company! Certainly we seemed to have demonstrated the truth of the adage, "Ole Virginny never tire." We had company, and we had company to eat with us, and enjoyed it.

Sometimes our guests were boys from camp who dropped in and took stewed apples or boiled peas, as the case might be. If we were particularly fortunate we offered a cup of tea sweetened with sugar. The soldier who dropped in always got a part - and the best part - of what we had. If things were scant we had smiles to make up for the lack of our larder, and to hide its bareness.

How we were pinched that winter! how often we were hungry! and how anxious and miserable we were! And yet what fun we had! The boys laughed at our crowded room and we laughed with them. After we bought our wood it was Robert E. Lee's adjutant who first observed the ends sticking out from under the bed; he was heartily amused and greatly impressed with the versatility of our resources.

"I confidently expect to come here some day and find a pig tied to the leg of the bed, and a brood or two of poultry utilizing waste space," said Colonel Taylor.

He wasn't so far out of the way, for we did get hold of a

lean chicken once some way or other, and we tied it to the foot of the bed, and tried to fatten it with boiled peas.

Wc devised many small ways for making a little money. We knit gloves and socks and sold them, and Miss Beth Sampson had some old pieces of ante-bellum silk that she made into neckties and sold for what she could get. For the rest, when we had no money, we went without those things which it took money to buy. With money a bit of meat now and then, a taste of sorghum, and even the rare luxury of a cup of tea sweetened with sugar, was possible. Without money, we had to depend upon the bags of peas, dried apples, or rice.

"If I ever keep house," said Miss Mary one day when we were getting supper ready, "there are three things which shall never come into it, rice, dried apples, and peas."

Mother was at the bureau slicing bread, Delia McArthur was setting the table, I was getting butter out of the firkin and making it into prints, and Miss Mary with gloves on - whenever she had anything to do she always put gloves on - was peeling and slicing tomatoes.

"I never want to hear of rice, dried apples, or peas again!" came from all sides of the room.

"If this war is ever at an end," sighed poor mother, "I hope I may sit down and eat at a decent table again. And I fervently hope that nobody will ever set a dish of rice, peas, or dried apples before me! If they do, I shall get up and leave the table."

"Me too," I piped. "Even if I didn't hate the things I should feel sensitive on the subject and take the offering of such a dish to me as a personal reflection."

One day we agreed to have a feast. The Sampsons were to bring their contributions, Miss Mary and Delia McArthur to put in theirs as usual, and mother and I to contribute our share, of course. Each of us had the privilege of inviting a friend to tea. Our room was chosen as the common supper-room because it had fewer things in it and was less crowded than the Sampsons'. The Sampsons, in addition to their coal-box, wood-pile, bags and barrels of provisions, had one more bed than we had, and also a piano. We had our tea-party and, guests and all, we had a merry time.

I never remember having more fun in my life than at the Arlington, where sometimes we were hungry, and while the country, up to our doors, bristled with bayonets, and the air we breathed shook with the thunder of guns.

For hungry and shabby as we were, crowded into our one room with bags of rice and peas, firkins of butter, a ton of coal, a small wood-pile, cooking utensils, and all of our personal property, we were not in despair. Our faith in Lee and his ragged, freezing, starving army amounted to a superstition. We cooked our rice and peas and dried apples, and hoped and prayed. By this time our bags took up little room. We had had a bag of potatoes, but it was nearly empty. there were only a few handfuls of dried apples left - and I must say that even in the face of starvation I was glad of that! - and there was a very small quantity of rice in our larder. We had more peas than anything else.

I had not heard from my husband for more than a week - indeed, there seems to have been in Richmond at this time a singular ignorance concerning our reverses around Petersburg. There were hunger and nakedness and death and pestilence and fire and sword everywhere, and we, fugitives from shot and shell, knew it well, but, somehow, we laughed and sang and played on the piano - and never believed in actual defeat and subjugation.

Sunday morning, the second of April, as President Davis sat in his pew at St. Paul's Church, a slip of paper was brought to him. He read it, quietly arose, and left the church.

General Lee advised the evacuation of Richmond by eight o'clock that night. That was what rumor told us at the Arlington. At first we did not believe it, but as that spring day wore on we were convinced. The Sabbath calm was changed to bustle and confusion - almost into riot. The streets were full of people hurrying in all directions, but chiefly in the direction of the Danville depot. Men, women, and children jostled each other in their haste to reach this spot. Loaded vehicles of every description rattled over the pavements.

During the day proclamation was made that all who wished could come to the Commissary Department and get anything they wanted in the way of provisions - without pay. I for one, in spite of my loathing for dried apples and peas, and a lively objection to starvation, would not entertain the thought at first. But the situation was serious. We discussed it in council, sitting around our room on beds; chairs, trunks, and the floor. We could not foresee the straits to which we might be brought. We considered that the evacuation of Richmond implied we knew not what. Unless we provided now by laying in some stores we might actually starve. Besides, Mrs. Sampson said she was just bound to have a whole barrel of flour, and she was going for it. That declaration wound up the conference. Mother said she would go with Mrs. Sampson, and I must needs go, I thought, to protect mother. We put on our bonnets - home-made straw trimmed with chicken feathers - and started. Such a crowd as we found ourselves in! such a starveling mob! I got frightened and sick, and mother and Mrs. Sampson were daunted. We had not gone many squares before we changed our course, and went to Mrs. Taylor's (Colonel Walter Taylor's mother) and I ran up the steps and asked her to lend us Bob, her youngest son, who was at home then, for our escort.

She and Bob explained regretfully that he could not serve us. Walter was to be married that day, and Bob had his hands full at home. "Married?" I cried in astonishment. I had known of his engagement, and that he expected to be married as soon as possible, but marrying at this crisis was incredible.

"Yes," said Bob. "I took the despatch to Betty while she was at church this morning. He told her to be ready and he would come to Richmond this afternoon for the ceremony. You see, General Lee is going to move the army west, and nobody knows for how long it will be gone, nor what will happen, and if Betty is married to Walter she can go to him if he gets hurt."

Of course, as Bob had to make all the necessary arrangements for the event his escort at the present moment was out of the question.

Somehow Mrs. Sampson managed to get her barrel of flour and have it brought to her room, but we didn't get anything.

That afternoon as I sat at my window I saw Walter ride up to the Crenshaws', where Betty was staying. He remained in the house just long enough for the ceremony to be performed, came out, sprang on his horse, and rode away rapidly.

President Davis and his Cabinet left Richmond that afternoon in a special train. Everybody who could go was going. We had no money to go with, though we did not know where we would have gone if the money had been forthcoming.

As darkness came upon the city confusion and disorder increased. People were running about everywhere with plunder and provisions. Barrels and boxes were rolled and tumbled about the streets as they had been all day. Barrels of liquor were broken open and the gutters ran with whisky and molasses. There were plenty of straggling soldiers about who had too much whisky, rough women had it plentifully, and many negroes were drunk. The air was filled with yells, curses, cries of distress, and horrid songs. No one in the house slept. We moved about between each other's rooms, talked in whispers, and tried to nerve ourselves for whatever might come. A greater part of the night I sat at my window.

In the pale dawn I saw a light shoot up from Shockoe Warehouse. Presently soldiers came running down the streets. Some carried balls of tar; some carried torches. As they ran they fired the balls of tar and pitched them onto the roofs of prominent houses and into the windows of public buildings and churches. I saw balls pitched on the roof of General R. E. Lee's home. As the day grew lighter I saw a Confederate soldier on horseback pause almost under my window. He wheeled and fired behind him; rode a short distance, wheeled and fired again; and so on, wheeling and firing as he went until he was out of sight. Coming up the street from that end toward which his fire had been directed and from which he had come, rode a body of men in blue uniforms. It was not a very large body, they rode slowly, and passed just beneath my window. Exactly at eight o'clock the Confederate flag that fluttered above the Capitol came down and the Stars and Stripes were run up. We knew what that meant! The song "On to Richmond!" was ended - Richmond was in the hands of the Federals. We covered our faces and cried aloud. All through the house was the sound of sobbing. It was as the house of mourning, the house of death.

Soon the streets were full of Federal troops, marching quietly along. The beautiful sunlight flashed back everywhere from Yankee bayonets. I saw negroes run out into the street and falling on their knees before the invaders hail them as their deliverers, embracing the knees of the horses, and almost preventing the troops from moving forward. It had been hard living and poor fare in Richmond for negroes as well as whites; and the negroes at this time believed the immediate blessings of freedom greater than they would or could be.

The saddest moment of my life was when I saw that Southern Cross dragged down and the Stars and Stripes run up above the Capitol. I am glad the Stars and Stripes are waving there now. But I am true to my old flag too, and as I tell this my heart turns sick with the supreme anguish of the moment when I saw it torn down from the height where valor had kept it waving for so long and at such cost.

Was it for this, I thought, that Jackson had fallen? for this that my brave, laughing Stuart was dead - dead and lying in his grave in Hollywood under the very shadow of that flag floating from the Capitol, in hearing of these bands playing triumphant airs as they marched through the streets of Richmond, in hearing of those shouts of victory? O my chevalier!

I had to thank God that the kindly sod hid you from all those sights and sounds so bitter to me then. I looked toward Hollywood with streaming eyes and thanked God for your sake. Was it to this end we had fought and starved and gone naked and cold? to this end that the wives and children of many a dear and gallant friend were husbandless and fatherless? to this end that our homes were in ruins, our State devastated? to this end that Lee and his footsore veterans were seeking the covert of the mountains?

Chapter XXVII

UNDER THE STARS AND STRIPES

THE Arlington is one-half of a double house, a veranda without division serving for both halves. Just before noon up rode a regiment of Yankees and quartered themselves next door. We could hear them moving about and talking, and rattling their sabers. But I must add that they were very quiet and orderly. There was no unnecessary noise. They all went out again, on duty, I suppose, leaving their baggage and servants behind them. They did not molest or disturb us in any way. After a while we heard a rap on the door, and on opening it three men entered. They were fully armed, and had come, as they said, to search the house for rebels. The one who undertook to search our rooms came quite in and closed the door while his companions went below. He was very drunk. Anxious to get rid of him quickly I helped him in his search.

He touched my arm and whispered: "Sis, I'm good Secesh as you - but don't say nothin' about it."

"You'd better look thoroughly," I insisted, pretending not to hear him.

Going to the bed I threw the mattress over so he could see that no one was concealed beneath. He followed and touched my arm again.

"Good Secesh as you is, sis. I ain't agwine to look into nothin', sis."

"There's nothing for you to find," I informed him, as I pulled a bureau drawer open for his inspection.

He waved it away with scorn. "I," he repeated, touching

his breast, "am good Secesh. Don't want to see nothin'. Don't you say nothin' - I'm good Secesh as you is, sis." I led the way into the next room to be searched, he following, asseverating in tipsy whispers, "Good Secesh as you is, sis," every few minutes.

We found little Ruf Pagett cleaning his gun.

"Better hide that, sonny," said our friend, glancing around. "That other fellow out there, he'll take it from you. But I won't take it from you. I won't take nothin'. I'm good Secesh as you is, bud. Hide your gun, bud."

Down-stairs our friends were having a harder time. The men who went through their rooms searched everywhere, and tumbled their things around outrageously. I could hear Mrs. Sampson quarreling. They went away, but returned to search again. She said she wouldn't stand it - she would report them. She saw General Weitzel and made her complaint, and he told her that the men were stragglers and had no authority for what they had done. If they could be found they would be punished. Before this time the fire had been brought under control. Houses not a square from us had been in flames. What saved us was an open space between us and the nearest house which had been on fire, and wet blankets. Mrs. Fry's son had had wet blankets spread over our roof for protection, and we had also kept wet blankets hung in our windows. At one time, however, cinders and smoke had blown into my room till the air was stifling and the danger great.

A niece of my husband's, a beautiful girl of eighteen, who had been ill with typhoid fever, had to be carried out of a burning house that night and laid on a cot in the street. She died in the street and I heard of other sick persons who died from the terror and exposure of that time.

As night came on many people were wandering about without shelter, amid blackened ruins. In the Square numbers were huddled for the night under improvised shelter or without any protection at all. But profound quiet reigned - the quiet of desolation as well as of order. The city had been put under martial law as soon as the Federals took possession; order and quiet had been quickly established and were well preserved. Our next-door neighbors were so quiet that with only a wall between we sometimes forgot their presence.

I must tell of one person who did not weep because the Yankees had come. That was a little girl in the house who clapped her hands and danced all around.

"The Yankees have come! the Yankees have come!" she shouted, "and now we'll get something to eat. I'm going to have pickles and molasses and oranges and cheese and nuts and candy until I have a fit and die."

She soon made acquaintances next door. The soldiers or their servants gave her what she asked for. She stuffed herself with what they gave her, and that night she had a fit and died, as she had said in jest she would, poor little soul!

That afternoon there was a funeral from the house, and all day there were burials going on in Hollywood.

Early on the morning of the third, when Miss Mary Pagett threw open her blinds, she beheld the gallery under her window lined with sleeping Yankees. When Delia McArthur and I went out for a walk we came upon Federal soldiers asleep on the sidewalks and everywhere there was a place for weary men to drop down and rest. In all this time of horror I don't think anything was much harder than making up our minds to "draw rations from the Yankees." We said we would not do it - we could not do it!

But as hunger gained upon us and starvation stared us in the face Mrs. Sampson rose up in her might!

"I'll take anything I can get out of the Yankees!" she exclaimed. "They haven't had any delicacy of feeling in taking everything we've got! I'm going for rations!"

So Mrs. Sampson nerved herself up to the point where she took quite a pleasure and pride in her mission. But not so with the rest of us. It was a bitter pill, hard, hard to swallow. Mother, to whose lot some species of martyrdom was always falling, elected to go with Mrs. Sampson. So forth sallied these old Virginia matrons to "draw rations from the Yankees." However, once on our way to humiliation we began to console ourselves with thoughts of the loaves and fishes. We would have enough to eat - sugar and tea and other delights! Presently mother and Mrs. Sampson returned, each with a dried codfish! There was disappointment and there was laughter. As each stately matron came marching in, holding her codfish at arm's length before her, Delia McArthur and I fell into each other's arms laughing. Besides the codfish, they had each a piece of fat, strong bacon about the size of a handkerchief folded once, and perhaps an inch thick. Now, we had had no meat for a great while, and we were completely worn out with dried apples and peas, so we immediately set about cooking our bacon. Having such a great dainty and rare luxury, we felt ourselves in a position to invite company to dinner. Mrs. Sampson invited half of the household to dine with her, and we invited the other half. Soon there was a great sputtering and a delicious smell issuing from the Sampsons' apartments and from ours.

Mother sliced the meat into the pan, and I sat on the floor and held it over the fire, while Delia spread the table. There was a pot on, which had to be stirred now and then. I, who always had a fertile brain in culinary matters, suggested that the potatoes - I neglected to state that a handful of potatoes had been dealt out with our rations - should be sliced very thin and dropped into the pan with the meat; and this done I fried them quite brown, taking much pains and pride in the achievement. Mother dished up the peas and set them on the table before our guests; and I passed around the fried meat and potatoes in the frying-pan, from which the company, with much grace and delicacy, helped themselves. Oh, how delicious it was!

As for the codfish, we had immediately hung that out of the window. The passer-by in the street below could behold it, dangling from its string, a melancholy and fragrant codfish. From Mrs. Sampson's window just below ours hung another melancholy codfish just like the one above it. We paid the old negress to do things for us with codfish - but not a whole codfish at a time. We cut off pieces of it, and so made good bargains, and one codfish go as far as possible. We had by this time got to a place where economy was not only a virtue but a necessity of the direst sort.

The last time I was in Richmond I took my children by the Arlington and pointed out to them the window from which our codfish hung.

And now Betty Taylor - Walter's bride - and I began planning to run through the Yankee lines together and join our husbands.

We did not think even then, you see, that the war was over. Our faith was still crediting superhuman powers to Lee and his skeleton army. Then there was President Davis's proclamation issued from Danville, wherein we found encouragement for hope. Then came the blow. We heard that Lee had surrendered. Lee surrendered! that couldn't be true! But even while we were refusing to believe it General Lee, accompanied, as I remember, by one or two members of his staff, rode up to his door. He bared his weary gray head to the people who gathered around him with greetings and passed into his house.

Hope was dead at last. But other things, precious and imperishable, remained to us and to our children - the things that make for loyalty and courage and endurance - an invincible faith - the enduring record of heroic example. Lee had surrendered, but Lee was still himself and our own - a heritage to be handed down by Americans to America when sectional distinctions have been swallowed up in the strength of a Union great enough to honor every son, whatever his creed, who has lived and died for "conscience' sake."

Sitting in my window that sorrowful day I saw three officers in gray uniforms galloping rapidly along Main Street. I recognized familiar figures in them all before they came as far as the Arlington. One turned out of Main Street, riding home to his wife, as I knew, before they reached the window; another did the same.

The third came galloping past.

I thrust my head out of the window.

"Walter!" I called.

He looked up.

"Hello, Nell!" he cried, waving his hat around his head and galloping on.

He was on his way to his bride from whom he had parted at the altar.

But even at this supreme moment of their lives he and Betty were good enough to remember me, and in a few hours after I hailed him from the window Walter called.

"Where is Dan?" was my first question.

"I don't know, Nell," he answered. "But I know he's alive and well and will be along in a few days."

That was all the comfort I got from any friends returning from the field.

A little later there was a grand review of Federal troops in Richmond, and I remember how well-clad and sleek they were and how new and glittering were their arms. Good boots, good hats, a whole suit of clothes to every man - a long, bright, prosperous-looking procession. On the sidewalk a poor Confederate in rags and bootless, stood looking wistfully on.

The next day I heard that General Rooney Lee had arrived, and I went to see him. I was shown up to his mother's room, and she told me that he had not come, but was hourly expected. When I called the next day I met him and Miss Mildred Lee in the door. They were going out, but the general stepped back with me into the hall.

"I came to see if you could tell me anything about Dan, general."

"Mrs. Grey," he said, "you know Dan as well as I do. He isn't whipped yet. I told him it was all foolishness, and that the war was over, but he wouldn't surrender with me, and is going through to Johnston's army. But he will have to come back, and he will be here soon, I think. Johnston's army has surrendered."

"You think then that nothing has happened to him, general?"

"Oh, no. I am sure of that." General Lee dropped his voice.

"Mrs. Grey, it may be several days before Dan gets in. In the meanwhile let me supply your wants as best I can. You should not mind applying to me or accepting assistance from me."

"I appreciate your kindness more than I can tell you, general, but I don't really need anything."

"If you should stand in need of money or assistance of any kind before Dan gets in, let me know, won't you?"

"Indeed I will, dear general."

We all three walked down Franklin Street together until Miss Mildred, who was going to see some friends on Grace Street, had to turn. After the two had just turned the corner I heard the general say:

"Wait for a minute, Mildred."

He slipped back, put his hand in his pocket, and took out a thin roll of bills, a very thin roll.

"Mrs. Grey," he said, "here is all the money I have in the world, ten dollars in greenbacks. Take half of it - I wish you would - it wouldn't inconvenience me at all. I will make some more soon, and then I will divide with you again until Dan comes home."

I could hardly speak for tears. At that moment I was richer than my general. I had at home in gold and greenbacks more money than General Lee.

"God bless you, general!" I managed to say.

"But really I don't need it. If I do really and truly I will come to you for it."

Franklin Street wasn't a good place to cry in, so I hurried home.

Still the days that passed did not bring me Dan. I became thoroughly miserable. I sat in my window and watched and was cross if anybody spoke to me.

One day a servant brought up a message:

"Er gent'man in de parlor to see yer, missy."

"What sort of a 'gent'man ' is it?" I asked tartly. There was but one man in the world I wanted to see or hear about just then.

"He ain't lak our people, missy. He's furrin - French or suppin nuther. He say how he usen ter know yer in Petersburg. An' how you lent 'im some - er - music - er suppin lak dat. An' he got - er - errah - suppin - I clar fo' de Lord, missy, I dunno what 'tis - but he got suppin - "

"Oh, I know," I said. "He's that old French music-teacher, and he's brought back that old music I lent him in the year one. Go tell him that I don't want it; he can have it."

Jake departed only to return in a more perplexed frame of mind and state of speech.

"He say how 'tain't no music he's got fur yer. He say - he do say, missy - but de Lord knows I dunno what he say! - but anyway be bleeged to see yer"

I got up and went down to the parlor in desperation.

Sure enough, it was the little French music-teacher, and he began apologies, acknowledgments and what not in his dreadful English.

"Madame, I haf no mooseek to you - not at all. I haf one message of you to ze majaire. If you not b'lief me," he fumbled in his pocket and brought out a dirty bit of paper, "look at ze cart - vat sall I call him? ze lettaire. If madame will look - I beg ze pardon of madame."

I snatched the paper out of his hand. And then - I couldn't make it out. Written in the first place with an indifferent pencil on a worn bit of the poor paper of that day and carried in the little Frenchman's very ragged and grimy pocket, the scrawl was illegible. It had never been more than a line of some five or six words. While I was trying to make it out the little Frenchman explained that it was merely a line introducing himself as the bearer of a message.

What that message was I never did hear, though the little Frenchman did his best to deliver and I to receive it. I got enough out of him, however, to know that Dan was well and on his way to Richmond. I also understood that he was not far from Richmond now, but what was detaining him I could not make out, though the little Frenchman, with many apologies, conveyed the hint to me that it was a delicate matter. After he was gone I wondered why I was so stupid as not to get the little man's address so that I could send some friends who understood French after him. From what he had said I had inferred that my husband would be with me the following day. I watched in a fever of impatience, but two days passed and no Dan.

The third night as I laid my aching head on the pillow I said: "Mother, if he don't come tomorrow, the next day I start out to look for him." Do you know how it is to feel in your sleep that some one is looking at you? This is the sort of sensation that aroused me the next morning, and I opened my eyes in the early dawn to find my husband standing by the bed with clasped hands looking down at me.

Ah, we were happy - we were happy! Ragged, defeated, broken, we but had each other and that was enough.

But there is a ludicrous side that I must tell you. I must explain how Dan was dressed. He wore a pair of threadbare gray trousers patched with blue; they were much too short for him, and there were holes which were not patched at all; he had no socks on, but wore a ragged shoe of one size on one foot, and on the other a boot of another size and ragged too; he had on a blue jacket much too small for him - it was conspicuously too short, and there was a wide margin between where it ended and his trousers began, and he had on a calico shirt that looked like pink peppermint candy. Set back on his head was an old hat, shot nearly all to pieces - you could look through the holes, and it had tags hanging around where the brim had been. He was a perfect old ragman except for the very new pink shirt.

"My dear Dan," I said, "what a perfect fright you are! What a dreadful ragtag and bobtail!"

"Why, Nell," he said, "I thought these very good clothes. What's missing, my dear? My suit is very complete; whole trousers, jacket, new shirt, hat on my head, even down to something on both feet. Last week I didn't have any shirt, nor any jacket to speak of, and my trousers weren't patched and I didn't have anything on my feet. One reason I took so long to get here was because I was trying to get a few clothes together - I wasn't dressed to my taste, you see. It took much time and labor to collect all this wearing apparel. I got first one piece and then another, until I am as you see me, fit to enter Richmond. Somebody stole my trousers one morning - I was in an awful plight. That was the time the little Frenchman passed and I sent you a message. Did he tell you that I'd get home as soon as I got another pair of trousers if somebody didn't steal my jacket by that time?"

I was laughing and crying all the time he was talking. When I pulled off boot and shoe I found that he had spoken the truth in jest when he said he had been walking barefoot nearly all the way. His feet were sore. I had some good shoes for him, and I got out an old civilian suit that he had worn before the war. It didn't fit him now and looked antiquated, but he donned it with great satisfaction.

Then we went out shopping. It was shopping in a city of ruins. As we walked along the streets there were smoking pits on each side of us. Here and there the remnants of what had been a store enabled us to purchase shoes at one place and the materials for two white shirts at another, and to our great joy we found a hat for which he paid two dollars, United States money.

We had nothing on which to begin life over again, but we were young and strong, and began it cheerily enough. We are prosperous now, our heads are nearly white; little grandchildren cluster about us and listen with interest to grandpapa's and grandmamma's tales of the days when they "fought and bled and died together." They can't understand how such nice people as the Yankees and ourselves ever could have fought each other. "It doesn't seem reasonable," says Nellie the third, who is engaged to a gentleman from Boston, where we sent her to cultivate her musical talents, but where she applied herself to other matters, "it doesn't seem reasonable, grandmamma, when you could just as easily have settled it all comfortably without any fighting. How glad I am I wasn't living then! How thankful I am that 'Old Glory' floats alike over North and South, now!"

And so am I, my darling, so am I!

But for us - for Dan and me we could almost as easily give up each other as those terrible, beloved days. They are the very fiber of us.

The End